REAL GHOST STORIES

OUIJA BOARD
HAUNTINGS

EVE S EVANS

ALSO BY

EVE S EVANS

Fiction:

The Haunting of Hartley House

Hartley House Homecoming

The Haunting of Crow House

The Haunting of Redburn Manor

Anthologies:

True Ghost Stories of First Responders

50 Terrifying Ghost Stories

Holiday Hauntings

Shadow People

Chilling Ghost Stories

Haunted Hotels

Haunted Hospitals

Haunted Objects

True Ghost Stories Haunted First Responders

For David

Follow Eve and her books on Goodreads or Bookbub! And get notified of any new reads coming in 2022-2023.

The following stories are based on true events.

CEMETERY

I have only had one experience using a Ouija board and that was enough for me to swear off the things for the rest of my life. I had been at a Halloween party with a few of my friends when they told me they had a cool idea and asked if I wanted to come along with them. When I asked them what they had in mind, all I got was "Don't worry, it will be fun." Not wanting to be left out I told them I was game for whatever.

As we drove away, they filled me in on the details of what they had in mind. One of them had bought a Ouija board earlier in the day. Their grand idea was to go to one of the local cemeteries and see if they could get it to work. So, besides trespassing, they wanted to mess with the spirits of the dead. Besides a dull party, this was on top of my priority list of things I wanted to do on Halloween.

I didn't want to look like the lame of the group, so I kept my mouth shut the entire way there. At this point, the worst thing I thought would happen that night was a possible misdemeanor on my record. I kept repeating the mantra, *we won't get caught. We won't get caught. Over and over in my head.* Still, it did little to settle the nerves that had twisted my stomach into a tight knot.

There was several small openings in the fence line on one side of the cemetery which allowed for easy access. The four of us made our way around the gravesites, taking care not to step on any. Looking back this seemed a little foolish considering we were there to stir up what we could with a Ouija board yet stepping on the gravesites was disrespectful.

One of my friends saw off to one side a bench

that mourners could use when visiting their deceased loved ones. This seemed like as good a place as any for what we had in mind, so we set the board on top of the bench and knelt around it. The ground was wet, which soaked the bottom half of my pants, another highlight to add to this evening.

I didn't know what to expect, but when the planchette started to move beneath my fingers I didn't expect the jolt of fear that went through me. Suddenly this was all too real, and it felt like we were doing something that we should be. Tempting fate if you will. We had come to their home, as uninvited guests.

Random letters that didn't spell anything at all kept appearing. I think too many things were coming through at the same time to make any sense. With the number of bodies in this cemetery, it was no wonder something like this was happening.

All four of us turned to look down the path we were next to when the sound of footsteps was moving towards us. I suddenly had images of me being hauled off in handcuffs and being shoved into the back of a police car. The sound got closer, but no figure seemed to appear out of the darkness. A rustle came from behind me, and I nearly jumped up and ran screaming out of there.

You could tell everyone was on edge. We weren't asking questions of the board but the planchette continued to move around selecting letters. A cold blast of air tickled the back of my neck, and I heard the distinct sound of someone breathing right behind me. Frozen in fear, I expected someone to reach out and touch me even though I knew no one was there.

I was so terrified I would have welcomed the police at that very moment. We'd started something that we had no business doing in the first place. No, I was worried that we'd gone too far to go back. Samantha, the one girl who'd come with us flinched, and the next second, she began to bawl her eyes out.

All of us just sat there, staring at her, unsure of what to do. With what I was experiencing, the cause could have been literally anything. Finally, I couldn't take it anymore. I pulled the planchette to the GOODBYE in the middle of the board and stood with my hands in front of me in supplication. I'd had enough of the entire thing.

My friends seemed to be in agreement because they were quick to take their hands from the device themselves. None of us wanted to touch the board so we just left it there on the bench while we tried to keep ourselves from running. Instead, we just ended up making an awkward fast walk back to our cars.

When we were finally safe inside and driven away, Samantha told us that she had felt someone grab her shoulder. Then she described a wave of sadness wash over her that she'd never experienced before. One by one we all shared our experiences, and with each tale I was sure what we'd done had been incredibly stupid. I know the Ouija board is simply a tool, but that night we used it in a form that it shouldn't.

FOUND

My husband Allen and I had just received the news that we were going to have our first child. The apartment that we currently lived in was too small to accommodate the new baby and we were in the market for a new house. The two of us were looking to get into a place before the baby was born thus, we were motivated to get the home buying process done quickly.

It took longer than expected but we finally found a nice ranch style house that was in our price range. Built in the late 60's, the home had some age to it, but a recent renovation had brightened up the place with a more modern open floorplan. Recently put on the market, we rushed to put in an offer in hopes of not getting into a bidding war with other potential buyers.

We were pleased when we found out a couple days later that the owners had accepted our price and after closing, we planned on moving into our new home in a few weeks. This felt like the first step we'd taken to creating the family we'd always talked about.

Moving day was quick to arrive and it felt like the two of us were running around trying to make sure everything went to plan. I was sure that we were going to forget something in the chaos, and the stress was making us both short with each other. Still, when we pulled up in front of our home all the weight seemed to fall off my shoulders. Even though I'd driven by nearly every day since we closed on the property, it seemed to exude a glow.

The movers made quick work of emptying the truck of the boxes and furniture from our old place. Our new place had a lot more room than the apartment we used to live in, and it felt like our meager possessions wouldn't even begin to fill the space. It was a little comforting knowing that the unpacking process wouldn't be such a monumental task though.

For the first few weeks it was a bit of a feeling out process. The sounds a new house makes that I wasn't used to seemed to bring me awake a few times a night. Between my fitful sleep and the pregnancy, I was constantly feeling worn down. I was becoming less and less of a help getting everything out of the boxes, but my husband never complained.

The day the final box was emptied was one we both felt like celebrating. We went out to dinner and planned on spending the evening watching a movie. Unfortunately, I was still exhausted and half an hour into the film my eyes were so heavy I knew I wasn't going to make it. I told my husband I was going to bed and left him to finish his movie. I was asleep the moment my head hit the pillow.

When I woke up to what sounded like footsteps coming from above me. My sleep starved brain was confused and struggled to make sense of the noise. We'd dealt with this same thing for the couple of years we lived in the apartment, and I momentarily forgot that's where I was. I turned over to see if the disturbance had woken up my husband and froze mid turn. *We didn't live in the apartment anymore.*

It was dark in the room and my husband's side of the bed hadn't been slept in. The longer I'd was awake the more problems with the noise I was having. Our home was only one story so it wasn't like it could just be Allen walking upstairs and it was far too late for him to be up in the attic moving around. I had a quick flash of a raccoon running around upstairs and groaned thinking about what damage it might be doing.

I walked out to the Livingroom to find out what happened to Allen coming to bed. As I suspected he was passed out on the couch with the television still on. I considered waking him up but decided to just turn off the TV and cover him with a blanket. I knew the pest problem wouldn't be fixed until the next day anyways.

He woke up uncomfortable and stiff, but his mood brightened after I fed him breakfast. It was my way to butter him up for what I was about to ask him to do. Allen was the kind of guy that was going to try and fix a problem before paying someone to do it. I knew not to argue with him about this because he was more likely to dig his heels in.

This was going to be the first time either of us had gone upstairs to inspect what the previous owners had left up here. I was a little apprehensive about encountering some sort of rabid animal, I was curious to poke around inside any boxes that were up there.

The attic's entrance was one of the old pulldown jobs with a hook. I followed him up through the narrow opening in the ceiling where he helped me onto the landing. We both clicked on our flashlights and swept the floor around us. To my chagrin, there were only a few cardboard boxes tucked away in one corner, other than that the floor was empty.

The other thing that was missing was any sign that an animal had been up here. There were no droppings anywhere and the floor was covered in a thick layer of dust on which a track would have been easily seen. Allen must have been thinking the same thing because he seemed to come to the same conclusion that there wasn't anything up here.

"Don't look at me like I'm crazy. I know what I heard." I told him.

He wigged his fingers at me. "Oooooooo.... Maybe this attic is haunted, and it was a ghost you heard up here."

He was trying to be funny, but I wasn't amused. He got that really quickly after seeing the face I made and to apologize helped me carry down the few boxes we'd found.

He set the boxes on the ground in the Livingroom and left me to hunt through them. The first of the boxes held nothing more than a few empty picture frames and a couple of old books. In the second one though I hit the jackpot. An old Ouija board and planchette had been wrapped within a sheet. There were a few chips and scratches here and there, but otherwise it was in pretty good shape given how old it appeared.

At this point, the last box had lost all interest for me. I'd ask Allen to try it out with me, but he didn't believe in ghosts or spirits so it would have been a waste of time. I did however have my friend Angie who was really into this kind of thing and would jump at the chance to use it with me. A quick phone call confirmed this, and we made plans to get together that night.

Allen didn't want any part of our "imaginary friends", so he and a couple friends went out to have an evening of their own. That just left me and Angie alone so we could concentrate without having to listen to his snide remarks.

This hadn't been the first time the two of us had used a Ouija board, but we were wary of this one in particular. I know well enough that objects can absorb the energy from a spirit. When dealing with an object like this that is used to channel spirits it is even more likely. To take precaution against any negative energies that may be attached we burned white sage over it.

We started by introducing ourselves and telling any spirits that were present that we were there to listen to them and offer our assistance if we could help. We moved the planchette in a circular pattern and then stopped it in the center of the board to wait for any message that would come through.

There was only a slight pause before the planchette began to move. Sometimes when using a Ouija board, the message is tough to understand, but when finished it was clear what the spirit was trying to tell us. G-E-T-O-U-T. The only question I had was why it wanted me to leave. When we asked the spirit again gave us a direct answer. M-I-N-E.

Now as much as the spirit would have liked us to comply with its wishes, which wasn't going to happen. This was my house now. As I saw it, that left me with two options. 1. Deal with the spirit living in my home or 2. Find a way for the spirit to move on. I didn't see a positive side to keeping the energy around that didn't want me here, so I chose option 2.

We tried with the Ouija board to ask the spirit why it wouldn't leave but all we got was a series of unintelligible letters that didn't seem to mean anything. Angie and I took this as the spirit was frustrated with us not agreeing to do as it asked. At this point I told the spirit directly that I had no intention of leaving. When I said this, I heard a distinct knocking sound above us.

"Is that you making that noise in the attic?" I asked. To which the planchette moved to the word YES. Given what we'd already been told, I figured it was safe to assume this had been the spirit who'd woken me up the night before.

I looked over to Angie hoping that maybe she would have an idea as to where we should go from here. She thought for a moment and then spoke. "Is there something of yours that's still here that's keeping you here?" The planchette moved again to the word YES. Angie continued, "Something that belonged to you?"

Again YES.

She looked over to me and I shrugged. The only things I'd found was the Ouija board and a few old picture frames. The idea that these things were keeping someone there seemed odd. Then I remembered there had been a third box that I hadn't looked through.

I told Angie I'd be right back and brought back the box that I hadn't looked through yet. There were a few old dolls that had seen better days, but at the bottom was a small jewelry box. I gently picked it up and opened the lid. Inside was a gold ring. It looked like one a man would get on his wedding day. If this was the case, it would be a deeply personal object and just the kind of thing that a spirit could attach to.

The only thing we had left to do was ask the spirit if this was his/her ring. When we did so the planchette immediately went to the word YES. It did this at least four times as if to punctuate the response. Now that we assumed we figured out the source of the spirit we had to do something about it. I could only think of one thing, return it to the family who it belonged.

We moved the planchette to the word GOODBYE and thanked the spirit for communicating with us, ending the session.

The following day I called the real estate agent and asked them to get in touch with the family whom we bought this house from. I told her that I believed they left something of value behind and I wanted to return it to them. A young man called me a few days later and did in fact confirm that the ring had belonged to his father who lived in this house until he died. We made plans to meet up so I could return it.

Up until the day that I returned the ring I would still hear what sounded like footsteps and creaking coming from the attic. Afterwards though, it has completely stopped. I wonder how long it would have gone on before I figured out what was happening if I hadn't found that Ouija board that day.

LOVE AFTER DEATH

A few years ago, my wife of thirty-six years, Evelyn, died suddenly of a brain aneurism. The doctors told me that there was nothing anyone could have done to save her. Thankfully she passed in her sleep and simply didn't wake up. For this I was very thankful, but it left me with a lot of unresolved feelings. I just couldn't move on with my life.

Even our room had been left untouched since that day like some kind of shrine to her. Our kids had been pushing me to get rid of her things, but it was just too painful. She had been the love of my life and I just wanted her back, those things were my way of holding on.

Finally at a loss for what to do, my daughter Susan suggested maybe I try and use a Ouija board in hopes of getting the closure I so desperately wanted. I'm not a person who subscribes to the supernatural aspects of life and was initially against such a thing. She pressed me though and finally just to get her off my back I agreed to try it.

Our anniversary was just a few weeks away, the first one since her passing, and I wasn't looking forward to it. Susan thought it was the perfect day to attempt communication because of the significance to both of us. I brought up some of my previous arguments against it, but again my reservations were overcome by her persistence. The date was set, and it seemed that we were going to do this whether I liked it or not.

As the date approached, I found myself growing more anxious at the prospect of talking to Evelyn again. It almost felt like I did when we went on our first date all those years ago. I didn't really know what I was supposed to wear for this sort of thing so I put on a casual suit thinking it would be appropriate. When Susan arrived at my door wearing jeans and a t-shirt I felt grossly overdressed. Her scrunching up her face and looking me up and down didn't help matters either.

We had a nice dinner and after we cleaned up, she brought out the board. I'd seen Ouija boards before in the stores, mass produced pieces made by game companies. This wasn't one of those. Susan had brought with her an intricately painted wooden board and planchette with a glass "eye" that would be used to indicate what letter the supposed spirit had selected. She told me that it was her own personal board and thought it might help us with what we were doing. The revelation that she owned such a thing was a surprise to me but given that she'd been the one to suggest this I guess I shouldn't have been.

We set up the board on top of the coffee table in the living room. After turning off the lights and lighting a few candles we sat on opposite sides of the table from one another and prepared to begin. She told me that it was important for me to take this seriously otherwise it would possibly keep us from getting the messages we were here to receive.

Susan asked me if I wanted her to direct the interactions. At this point all I could do was nod affirmative. I admit that I was afraid, not of what we were doing, but that Evelyn wouldn't show up. I'd gotten my hopes up so high, if nothing happened it would be a huge disappointment.

We placed our hands on the planchette and Susan started off by making several figure eight patterns with it and stating that we had gathered with good intentions. In a commanding voice she said that no negative energies were welcome and that we were there to communicate with Evelyn, her mother and my wife. She asked her to come forward in order to for those of us she left behind to gain the closure that we all needed.

The two of us sat there and waited for what seemed like a long time but my faith in Evelyn kept me from throwing my hands up in frustration. Susan reached out again, imploring her to come and speak with us, yet the planchette still didn't move. I was losing hope, I looked up and met my daughter's eyes. I could see how much this was hurting her too.

I never meant to say anything during this whole thing, but I felt compelled to speak up. "Ev, sweetheart, it's me. I don't know if you can hear me, but I really need you with me right now."

I was able to hold Susan's gaze for only a moment, then my eyes fell towards the board. The planchette started to slide along the board and spelled out the word LOVE. Just that word had tears streaming out of both eyes. I couldn't believe that I'd waited so long to do this, and all out of stubborn disbelief.

For the next fifteen minutes I Evelyn confirmed to me that she was okay and that she was sorry that she left so abruptly. She apologized for the way it happened, but she'd came to accept that it was her time and hoped I could do so as well.

Her final message to me is what was the most impactful. It came as a single word, but I knew immediately what it meant. FOREVER was the word she told me. Evelyn was letting me know that no matter how long we were apart that our love would last an eternity. I believed her whole heartedly. I now know I'll see my love again. Our time hasn't come to an end, but rather just been put on pause.

WHISPERS

A few years ago, I went to a psychic medium in hopes of contacting my dad's spirit. He had died when I was young and I was seeking out his approval for the choices I'd made in my life, especially those as a parent. He'd done so much for us, and I'd tried to walk in his footsteps if not fill his shoes.

Even though I was told that there were no guarantees that he would make himself known, I had high hopes that he would come forward. We'd always shared a strong connection while he was alive and I was sure he'd answer my call, even after all the time that had passed. The woman had in fact been able to give me some messages, but when the time for the session ended, I found myself wanting to ask more questions.

Now that I had established his willingness to make contact, I felt comfortable trying to seek out answers on my own. I don't possess any psychic abilities of my own, so I was relegated to using a Ouija board in hopes of communicating with my departed father. Even though I was a firm believer in the spiritual realm, I had my doubts as to the power of a mass-produced item such as the one I was going to use.

I reached out and asked my mother and sister to aid in my goals. I figured that soliciting people that were close to him would only help draw him to us. Both of them are also believers in the supernatural and had been the ones who suggested I seek the help of the medium in the first place, so when I asked for their help they were quick to agree.

We agreed to meet at my mom's house, again a choice based on it was the same place where I grew up and the last place dad called home. After a quick discussion we chose Saturday night as the time in which all of us would attempt to contact him.

After we hung up it was like time decided to move at half speed. Work seemed to drag on and the television shows that I normally found escape through seemed to not be able to hold my interest. The possibility of talking to my dad again seemed to have taken up residence in my mind and nothing could distract me for more than a moment or two.

Despite its best attempt, the week did finally come to an end and the three of us were sitting around my mom's dining room table. We'd turned off all the lights in the room and lit a few candles that we'd gathered from various parts of the house. The board sat out on the table, waiting for us to begin.

I had to admit, even if we weren't able to make contact with my dad, the room definitely looked the part for what we planned on doing that night. Unbidden, a tremor passed though me. We were here with the best of intentions, but I had to admit, the atmosphere was more than a little creepy.

Before we began, my mom placed the ring she gave him when they were married on the board. This had been planned in order to help draw him to us. Afterwards, all of us placed our hands on top of the planchette and stated to the spirits of the house that we were closing this gathering to any spirits who meant us any harm. Next, we moved the pointer in a circular pattern and said that we were reaching out to the spirit of my dad.

I sat there with my fingers lightly on the planchette while my eyes bore holes through the board in front of me. My eyes started to burn as I refused to blink fearing that I might miss the slightest hint that he was here with us. Seconds continued to tick by, but nothing happened. I felt my hope beginning to wane. I distinctly remember thinking; *this is what I got for believing this piece of cardboard and plastic would let me talk to my dad.*

I started to feel a tightening in my chest and my heart began to beat noticeably faster. When the planchette first moved it was so slight I almost thought I'd imagined it. Then it moved again, and I had to hold back a gasp. Hope bloomed in me for an instant, then threatened to extinguish just as fast when I looked at the two other women with me. They were so focused on what was happening that I didn't think there was any way they could have done it themselves.

The pointer moved smoothly over the board as it selected six letters: F-A-M-I-L-Y. When it concluded the final letter, I felt a tear run down my cheek. To overcome with emotion my sister asked the only question that mattered at that point. "Dad, is that you?"

The planchette didn't hesitate for a moment before it made its way over to YES. I asked him if he was okay and the device made a circle back to the word YES.

For the next hour it was like we were having a conversation, although it was in an unconventional manner. Dad continued to assure us that he was always with us, especially in the most important parts of our lives. He even thanked my sister for naming her four-month-old son after him. This revelation brought about quiet sobs from her which required a stoppage until she could regain her composure.

The emotions of the experience were taking their toll on all of us. I could have sat there at the table for hours, but my body was already begging for sleep. Mom especially looked like she was about to fall asleep where she sat. I told my dad that we were going to go but wanted him to know that we missed him dearly and loved him very much. That is when the most amazing part of the evening happened.

"I love you." It was only a whisper, but I still knew the sound of my dad's voice.

My eyes shot open, and for a moment all of the fatigue I'd been feeling suddenly vanished. The voice had been so quiet, and I almost didn't believe that it had actually happened. I looked up and saw startled expressions on my mom and sister's faces. I wanted to tell them what had happened, but I couldn't bring myself to speak, but doing so felt like a betrayal. This was a message just for me, and me alone.

I like to believe that all of us received a similar message that night. It was a moment of healing and closure for all of us. Dad was taken from all of us far too soon and it was his way of telling us that he is proud and loves all of us. Since that night we have tried to contact his spirit, but the planchette has remained still. If the whisper he spoke in my ear is the last thing that I hear from my dad, I can't think of anything that I would have wanted to hear more.

THE ROBED FIGURE

While I was still in high school I kind of went through a goth faze. I don't really know what the cause of it was, maybe I was dealing with some depression or just normal teenage angst, but something about the lifestyle called to me. I had gone all in on it, the makeup, literature, new friends. My parents were supportive of my new choices, although it probably killed my mom to do so.

One night me and one of my friends were spending the night at her house when she brought out a Ouija board. While reading, I'd heard of these things before and the power that they possessed if used. When she asked me if I wanted to try it, I quickly jumped at the chance. The supernatural had always interested me, even before my shift to goth.

Erica turned off all the lights in her room and lit a couple of black candles that she told me she had for just this type of thing. Right from the beginning we started receiving messages. Most of which were mundane things, random names and numbers that didn't seem to have any meaning. It was when we started asking things about our future when they started to take a darker turn.

I had just finished asking what the name of the guy I would marry. The planchette seemed content to move in a slow circular pattern on the board without spelling anything out. I looked up at Erica to see if she had something to ask. My eyes froze, her eyes had rolled back and the only thing that I could see was the white parts. Even though she seemed to be in some sort of a daze, her mouth was forming words though she wasn't actually speaking.

A movement behind her caught my attention and I saw what looked like her shadow growing up towards the ceiling. Fear clouded my judgement, and it took me a moment to figure out what I was supposed to do. I quickly moved the pointer towards the goodbye part of the board. The flames of the candles flicked slightly, and Erica seemed to collapse to her side.

For a moment I thought she had died. She was so still, and her face was even paler than before, which given her already pallor skin was terrifying. Then her chest rose and fell, and I was able to release a breath I didn't even know I was holding. She was at least alive and at the moment that was all I cared about.

She came to slowly at first but once her eyes opened up, she recovered really quickly. Erica told me she remembered feeling really cold all of a sudden and the next thing she was waking up on the floor of her bedroom. Once I got her settled into her bed and she had fallen asleep I excused myself and drove home.

I arrived shortly before midnight. The emotions of the evening had drained me, and I was asleep moments after I crawled into bed. Exhaustion didn't save me from the fitful dreams that plagued me though. I saw Erica with her eyes rolled back into her skull, but this time I could hear her speaking a strange language as she swayed back and forth.

I woke up screaming, my throat horse from the strain. I didn't know how long I'd been doing it, but I was surprised the noise hadn't roused my parents to at least check on me. When I looked towards my door, I noticed a robed figure that stood about three- or four-feet tall staring at me. It didn't have any features, just a general shape that was formed out of the shadows themselves.

I went to scream for help when I felt an incredible force bin me down onto the bed. The weight of it was so great I felt like I couldn't breathe. My muscles struggled to contract, allowing me to take in the necessary oxygen, but I wasn't strong enough. My lungs were burning, and my vision was starting to tunnel. A high pitch buzzing sound seemed to be coming from everywhere.

I'm going to die. I was absolutely sure of it. I had no way of fighting this thing in front of me. Just before I lost consciousness, the weight suddenly came off me. I sucked in a deep breath, the air was cold, and it burned on the way down. I didn't care though; I was so desperate to breathe that I welcomed the sensation.

After a few minutes the ringing sound faded from my ears, and I didn't feel like I was going to suffocate right there in my bed. The figure at the end of my bed was gone almost like it hadn't been there at all. If it weren't for the fact, I'd almost died I would have questioned whether I'd even seen something or if it was just a hallucination.

The only thing that I think could have brought the robed figure to my room was the Ouija board. We'd opened ourselves up to communicating with things that didn't belong in our world. It was us that were to blame. We let it in.

LUCIFER

Lucifer. The Fallen Angel. For as long as I can remember I have been interested in him. When I was younger, I had numerous experiences I could not explain that got me thinking one thing. Lucifer.

My family had just moved into a new house, I was in my room doing my homework and I heard my name being called. It sounded like my mom. So, I went downstairs and said, "Yeah?"

She looked at me all weird and said, "Yeah what?"

"You called me. What did you want?"

She shook her head no. "I didn't call you. I was doing dishes."

I shrugged it off and went back upstairs. Only thing is this happened up until I moved out at 18. After a while I just quit answering when my name was called.

I was in bed one night; I was having a somewhat disturbing dream. When I awoke, I was pinned to the bed? I could not see anything there, but I felt pinned as if something would not let me up. I have read on this and am aware of sleep paralysis. So, it is possible that may be what it was. But I w. not forget how it felt. Not like being paralyzed. It felt like something was holding my arms and legs in place.

I had a friend over because we were doing an assignment together in high school English class. We were studying in my room, and I had to go to the bathroom.

When I got back, she was all nervous looking and as white as a sheet. I asked her what was wrong, and she said she heard whispering while I was gone coming from my closet.

Needless to say, she left without telling me what any of the whispers said. I still do not know to this day.

Another friend of mine I confided in. They were into horror stuff and the paranormal so I figured if anyone could give me answers or direction, Sarah could.

Sarah came over for a sleepover and brought her Ouija board so we could attempt to contact the spirit(s) that seemed to be haunting me.

Once we started asking questions, I started to get nervous. Some of the answers were raising the hair on my arms and causing me to sweat. Should I be doing this? Am I opening a door I will not know how to close? I wish those thoughts went through my mind that night... but they did not.

Is there anyone here with us?

YES

Are you a spirit?

NO

Are you a demon?

YES

Are your intentions bad?

NO

Are you lying?

YES

What is your name?

KILPIN

Kilpin, is this what we should call you?

YES

Do you call my friend's name?

YES

Why?

(No answer)

Did you pin my friend to the bed?

NO

Then who did?

(a bunch of random letters that meant nothing)

You are lying. It was you, wasn't it?

YES

Did you ever whisper in my friend's closet?

NO

Then who did?

(a bunch of random letters that mean nothing)

You are a just a liar. It was you, wasn't it?

YES

Why are you here?

(No answer)

Are you Lucifer?

(The planchette started going to YES but instead fell down to GOODBYE)

We figured that that was that. Demon was done talking. Did I feel much better after this "session"? Umm no. If anything, I felt like it brought up more questions. Was there really a demon in my house? And if so, why did he like messing with me? I thought back over my entire life. There was nothing I had done to anyone to deserve a demon attaching itself to me.

Sarah and I put the board on top of my bed while we sat beside my bed on the floor talking about boys from school. After about ten minutes, the board fell off the bed almost right into our laps.

We stared at each other both of our mouths open wide. "I put that board in the middle of my bed," I said.

"So, it should not have been able to fall off," she finished for me.

I nodded.

"Should we try again?" She asked. "Maybe it wants to talk some more."

Again, we sat around the board and waited.

Did you want to talk with us?

YES

What is your name?

(No response)

We would like to know your name so we can call you by it when we ask questions.

NO

Sarah shivered heavily then looked over her left shoulder.

Are you breathing on my neck?

YES

She looked at me her eyes wide and my heart started pumping so loudly I thought she could hear it too.

What do you want to talk about?

LOCK

What about a lock?

(No response)

I do not understand what lock means.

(No response)

Then I felt like something was touching the back of my shirt. Like the feeling when a breeze picks up at it just softly sways with it.

Are you touching my back?

NO

Are you breathing on my back?

YES

Sarah and I exchanged glances. I was pretty much done with it all at that point. If it could breathe on me, I didn't want to know what else it could do. But Sarah wasn't done yet.

Give us a sign that you are in the room with us.

(No response)

Ok then… I guess we are going to say 'goodbye'…

A clank against my headboard.

We stared at each other. We decided it best to say goodbye. And we did.

After that night I still had the occasional paranormal thing happen, but not as many as before. So, I don't know if by having that conversation with whatever it was calmed things down or what.

I was never 'pinned down' to my bed again after that night. I also never heard the phantom voices calling my name either. Some say as you age the paranormal doesn't affect you as much as when you are a child. So maybe that's it? I grew up and things just quit happening as much.

FRIENDS FOREVER

Recently my husband and I had a few friends over for a night of wine and binging some episodes on HBO. We had dropped our son off at my mom's house so we could stay up late and be a little rowdy without risk of keeping him up all night. It had been a while since I'd had a kid free night and I was looking forward to it.

Unfortunately luck wasn't on our side. Thunderstorms had blown into the area and a transformer nearby ended up getting struck by lightning. The power was cut off, and we had a decision to make as to what the rest of our evening would consist of. We were about to call it a night when I brought the idea up of bringing out an old Ouija board that I had. Everyone else seemed like they were game to try so we pulled out some candles to set the mood and I grabbed the board out of a closet.

The whole thing seemed a little silly, we weren't teenagers anymore. This was the kind of thing we should have outgrown a long time ago, believing in ghosts and demons. Still, when I sat there and looked at the planchette sitting there in the middle, I couldn't suppress the shiver that passed through me. There was a number of occasions that were more than a little creepy when I'd used boards just like this in the past.

All four of us placed our hands on the planchette and moved it around in a circular pattern while stating that we were looking to make contact with any spirits who were wanting to speak with us. All of a sudden, the device jerked up towards the word NO. I looked around and saw my husband smiling and I knew that he'd moved the pointer intentionally. I gave him a kick in the shin under the table and told him to be serious.

We returned our hands to their positions, and I asked again if there were any spirits out there that wanted to talk to us. The planchette moved to the word YES and stopped. My eyes shot towards my husband expecting he'd moved it again, but he just shook his head. My friends also gave me similar responses.

I know I hadn't moved it, so I went on with the next question. I asked what the name of the spirit whom we were communicating with was. It spelled out T-Y-L-E-R.

We went on to ask a few other questions like when he died and how it happened but all we ever got was random letters that never seemed to make any sense. If this was a spirit we were communicating with, it just didn't seem to be able to give us any answers we could understand. Because of this, our interest in continuing quickly waned and we told the spirit goodbye.

The next day my husband went over to my

mom's to pick up our son and I went to run a few errands. After a few hours I got back, and my husband was in the living room watching some sort of sporting event on television and I could hear my son upstairs. I could hear him talking and figured maybe one of his friends had come over to the house.

I asked my husband who he was talking to, and his response was that he'd been up there talking to himself for almost an hour now. For some kids this would have been normal, but not our son. If he was playing by himself, he tended to be quiet.

I wanted to say hello to him and make sure he was okay since I hadn't seen him since the night before, so I went upstairs to his room. Not only was he sitting there talking to himself, but he didn't have any toys out. he was just sitting there facing one of the corners to his room.

I can't tell you how much this behavior upset me. He was seven years old, still within the stages where he could have an imaginary friend, but he was an outgoing young boy with a lot of friends at school. Because of this, this type of thing seemed out of place. I walked in and he didn't even seem to notice I was there. He just sat there with his back to me totally engrossed in the corner.

"Hi mom."

I stopped a few steps from him. I didn't know how he'd known I was even there. I hadn't said anything to him, but it was possible he assumed it was me from the garage door opening. "Hey Sammy, what are you doing up here?" I asked him.

He finally turned around to look at me. "Nothin'"

"Who are you talking to?" I asked him to get to the point.

"My new friend," he said.

At that point I just assumed he had created an imaginary friend. "Does your friend have a name?"

He gave me a big grin. "His name is Tyler."

Something about that particular name gave me pause. I knew I'd heard it somewhere, but I couldn't place it for a few seconds. Suddenly the pieces to the puzzle seemed to lock into place and I remembered the name from the Ouija board the night before. The spirit had said its name was Tyler. Now my son was telling me that he was talking to an imaginary friend with the same name...

I left him in his room and went down to talk with my husband about what Sammy had told me. He brushed it off as just a coincidence, but I wasn't satisfied with that response. The idea that I'd invited something into our home that was now talking to our son left a sinking feeling in my stomach.

Over the next week Sammy continued to talk to Tyler more and more. By day seven both my husband and I had caught him awake in the middle of the night talking to a seemingly empty room. Every time though he would claim to be talking to his friend Tyler.

When I asked him to draw a picture of Tyler for me, he told me that it was against the rules, and he'd promised not to let anyone know what Tyler looked like. When he went to school though I went through his room and found some disturbing drawings of a large black shape that seemed to be wearing a top hat. That was the day I made an appointment with a child psychologist for the following afternoon.

When we went, he asked to leave him alone with Sammy. As much as I wanted to hear what was being said, I agreed. After about fifteen minutes he came back and told me that he believed that Sammy created Tyler in response to an unknown issue at school. I wasn't so sure.

I scheduled another appointment for a couple of weeks from that day and thanked him for his time. We continued to go to see the doctor for a few months, but Tyler remained a constant presence in our house. At this point I'm starting to worry that he may never leave my son alone, the real worry is that Sammy doesn't seem to want him to. When he calls Tyler his "Best Friend" it sends a chill through my entire body.

SLEEP OVER

My four friends and I were spending the night together in order to celebrate Christina's birthday. Her parent's had gone to stay at a hotel for the evening so the five of us could have the house to ourselves, so we didn't have that feeling of them watching over us constantly. We'd ordered some sushi and rented some horror flicks in hopes of scaring ourselves a little bit.

After watching one of the movies all of us realized we had seen far too many of these types of films. The stories may be different, but in the end too many of them were predicable. Part of being scared is the unknown or the possibility that it could *actually* happen.

Christina must have been reading my mind because all of a sudden, she flicked off the movie. "This is boring."

There was quiet noises of accent around the room. What was the point of having a house to yourself if you didn't take advantage of it? None of us were into drinking, not that we were old enough anyways, and we didn't really have any good ideas to go anywhere.

Carly all of a sudden got a look in her eye. "Hold on a second, I'll be right back."

She walked out the front door leaving the rest of us looking at each other, confused. When she came back, she was holding a box against her chest. "I thought maybe tonight we could try this."

She turned the box around and I could see that it was a Ouija board. I'd never tried one before and hadn't every planned on it either. I wasn't into the occult and thought that the stories I'd heard about these things were just made up. I seemed to be the only one though since the others were quick to agree.

Christina went and grabbed some candles and the five of us circled around the board. The instructions said that we had to all place a hand onto the planchette and make a figure eight with it five times to begin. After doing this we waited for it to move. The planchette didn't move though, it just sat there in the middle of the board.

"I think we're supposed to ask it a question," Jessica said.

The most obvious one seemed to be whether a spirit was there with us. When we asked though, nothing happened. My beliefs of these things were quickly becoming confirmed as a hoax, but I was willing to play along for the sake of my friends.

They asked question after question, only to be ignored by any spirits, real or otherwise in the house. I could tell that everyone was getting frustrated. I'd already thought this was going to be a waste of time when all of a sudden, the planchette started to slide in a slow jerky fashion across the board. My first thought was that this was one of the other girls doing this in order to have *something* happen. After all, there hadn't been any movement for the last twenty minutes.

I looked up, trying to figure out who was the one moving it by their faces, but they seemed as perplexed as I was. The one thing I knew for sure is I wasn't the one pushing it. I watched as it spelled out random letters that didn't seem to make any sense. Then the pointer went back to the center of the board and stopped.

All of us looked at each other, but none of us spoke for a few seconds. Finally, Trina broke the silence. "Okay, which one of you did that?" To her question all four of us shook our heads that we didn't. "Well, it wasn't me," she said quietly.

Since the planchette had moved, there had been a strange feeling in the pit of my stomach, a heaviness that had yet to abate. Carly asked again if someone was there, and the pointer moved slowly to the word YES. One of the other girls let out a nervous giggle, but I didn't see who it was.

I was starting to get a little freaked out. This was supposed to be fun, but it didn't feel *fun*. It felt like someone was standing right behind me, hovering just over my shoulder. Christina asked if this thing that was speaking to us was dead. That is when the planchette pointed to NO.

The answer was confusing, I didn't know how a spirit could be communicating with us if it wasn't dead. Jessica asked it what its name was after which it pointed to NO.

"You won't tell us your name. Is that what you're saying?" she asked.

The planchette started making large circles. It moved faster and faster which I took for this spirit getting angry. Finally, it stopped suddenly on the word YES. The fact that it wouldn't tell us a name felt like a bad sign. What reason would it have to keep this from us.

The bad feeling in my stomach had only intensified. I hadn't yet spoken a question but there was something that I felt compelled to ask. I was afraid to know the answer though. Before I could chicken out, I blurted it out. "Where are you?"

The planchette started making fast circles again and then started to spell out letters. I-N-H-E-L-L-I-N-H-E-L-L-I-N-H-E-L-L

Over and over again it spelled the same letters out. It moved from one to the next faster and faster until it was all we could do to keep our hands on the device. Finally, it moved back to the center of the board and stayed still. The pause almost felt worse than the motion, the feeling of something looming over the top of me was almost unbearable.

Christina started to ask a question. "Are you saying you're a demo..."

Even before the word demon could be spoken, a

loud bang came from somewhere behind her. It came so suddenly that all of us pulled our hands away from the planchette. All of us looked around, but none of us indicated that we saw anything.

"We have to say goodbye," Carley said to all of us. I could tell she was afraid. Frankly, I was way past that.

I reached out with the others and touched the device. It started making angry circles again, obviously upset by our intention to stop talking to it. Undeterred though, we all said goodbye at the same time and the planchette stopped.

The five of us sat there quietly trying to figure out what to say about what just happened. Was it a demon that had contacted us or was it just our subconscious minds moving it? Either way, I was done playing with the board and messing around with powers I didn't understand. If I never seen one of the boards again it would be fine by me.

G-E-T-O-U-T

A few years ago me and a couple of friends moved into an apartment together. All of us were going to college and it was a way for the three of us to save a little money on our living expenses and at least we would know the people who shared the house with. It took us about a month, but finally we found a house that all of us could afford and shortly thereafter the rental agreement was signed.

From the very beginning of us living their strange things would seem to happen. Doors would open and close on their own, strange knocking sounds could be heard during various times of the day, even our personal possessions would go missing only to show up in places where they hadn't been before.

At first, we chalked these things up to forgetfulness or strange pressure changes in the house. Sure, there was the occasional joke that we had inherited a ghostly roommate when we moved in, but those comments were all in jest.

As time went on the occurrences seemed to happen more often. The doors wouldn't just click shut, but slam closed when one of us was alone. This was also about the time when I started to get the feeling like somebody was always following me no matter where I went while I was home. As soon as I'd leave the sensation would dissipate only to return when I did. We'd even stopped making the lighthearted comments about a ghost in the house, with everything that was going on, none of us thought it was funny.

My grades had begun to slip in my classes and my relationships with my friends and family had suffered as well. My mom had constantly been asking me if something was wrong, but I didn't really know how to break the news to her that I thought my house was haunted. She didn't believe in such things, and I wasn't in the mood for a lecture on stress management.

Things had come to a head when we were taking mid-terms. We still had eight months left on our lease, but the prospect of paying a penalty was something we'd all discussed in order to escape whatever was going on. Even with all of us living there, money was still somewhat tight and the amount we'd have to pay felt daunting. That is when Greg suggested we try using a Ouija board in order to see if there was something that could be done to help whatever this spirit was leave the house.

This option seemed reasonable, but there was a part of me that hesitated before readily agreeing to it. I'd heard stories where using a Ouija board had made things worse. So far none of us had been physically hurt, it had been contained to just noises, doors moving on their own and the feeling of being watched. Still, it was unnerving, and I was getting to my wits end. Finally, I agreed that it was something we should try.

The next day Greg went out and bought the Ouija board, but we didn't immediately jump into it. I think the three of us were having second thoughts as to what could happen if we took that next step. After a particularly upsetting night where the activity had kept us, all awake the entire night, we finally decide the time had come to either do something about it or leave.

That night the three of us sat around our kitchen table with the board sitting between us. There was a part of me that still didn't want to do this. There was a part of me that expected the planchette to start moving on its own with all of the activity we'd experienced while we had lived here. Maybe I was just hoping it would, so I didn't have to touch it. It felt like by touching it we would be crossing a line from which we couldn't go back from.

Despite my better judgement all of us put our hands on the pointer and moved it around in a circle like we were instructed to do. I didn't know how long we were supposed to wait for something to happen but as soon as I asked if there were any spirits who wanted to communicate with us it immediately went to YES. If I hadn't seen and heard all that I had in the past few months, I would have been sure one of the other two had moved it themselves. Now though, I didn't even question what was happening.

We asked a few basic questions and established that we were communicating with the spirit of an elderly woman who claimed to have died in the house. When we asked her if she was the only one who was here in the house the planchette rushed to the word NO. The next question we asked her was, "Is the other entity here with us?", in which she responded NO.

Greg was the next to ask. "Is the other spirit evil?" When the pointer slid immediately to the word YES, a chill went down my spine. This was what I'd been afraid of. I'd always suspected this was the case, but to have it confirmed only made me dislike what had been happening that much more. I no longer could trust that the thing we were talking to wasn't the evil entity itself. What would stop it from lying to us in order to deceive us?

Knowing we were dealing with something evil, we started asking questions about what it was and its name. We didn't get any real answer to these questions but were able to establish that it would hurt us if it could. There was one final question that I felt needed to be asked, if we were going to still live here, we needed to know if there was a way to get this evil spirit to leave.

"What are we supposed to do?" I asked. The planchette moved and began to spell, G-E-T-O-U-T. It continued to say the same thing, even when we tried asking something else. It continued to tell us to get out of the house. With no other answers seemingly coming we closed the session by moving the pointer to goodbye.

Even though this wasn't the answer we wanted, it was an answer. The next day the three of us informed the landlord we would be leaving and were aware that we'd have to pay the penalty for doing so. Honestly it was the best $1000 I'd ever spent. So far it doesn't appear that the evil spirit has followed any of us to our new places, and I can only hope it stays that way.

ANSWER IT

When we were kids back in the 90's, we heard the stories. Stories of Demons and possessions and evil entities coming through Ouija boards. We didn't believe that by any means they could be real. I mean how is a board supposed to let in a Demon.

So naturally, a few of my friends and I got a Ouija board and wanted to try our luck at contacting a spirit.

Amy, Jen, Trevor and I sat around the board. We read the instructions out loud and began to follow the steps.

We seemed to contact a spirit named Mickey. I honestly thought someone was making this up because the name was part of a popular cartoon.

Mickey seemed to not like me at all.

Because we all still weren't convinced this was an actual spirit and not one of us moving the planchette, we decided to make Mickey talk to me even though he didn't want to.

We all brought our hands to the planchette. Mine were the closest and when they came within an inch of it, the planchette moved to the other side of the board. Everyone's hands were above the board. So, it could not have been a magnet. It gave me chills.

After that, the planchette refused to move for any of us. So instead of all of us, we took turns trying to calm Mickey down.

Jen got on it first. Mickey said he was angry. He told us to listen. We all sat there in silence for a minute or two then shrugged it off. Listen for what? That's when the phone on the wall rang. No joke.

We all stared over at it as it rang and rang and rang. Then after over ten rings, Amy nudged me.

"Go answer it," She instructed.

I took a deep breath, got off the carpet and walked over to the phone.   By now it was on its twentieth ring. Who would be calling that would be willing to let it ring so long?

I pulled the receiver from its cradle and listened. The others huddled around me in a circle trying to overhear.

On the other hand, it was static. Except what sounded like bugs. Like thousands of bugs scrabbling around.

Then it sounded as if something was trying to whisper something through the static, but we were unable to understand it.

I hung up the phone.

We all just stared at each other, silent.

"Whelp," Jen said picking up her bag, "I think I'm going to head home."

"Ya, me too," said Amy.

Trevor paused after the others left. He seemed to look guilty. "You going to be ok by yourself?"

I looked around the room, "Ya, my parents will be home soon."

He grabbed up his bag and waved, "Ok. See you at school on Monday."

"Bye."

I watched out the window as they all walked down the street. Outside the sun was setting and the streetlamps were just illuminating the darkness.

I turned to face the living room and the board that still sat on the coffee table. I drew in a deep breath and willed myself forward. When I reached the board, I paused before putting it back in its box. I guess some part of me expected the planchette to just move wildly about, but it didn't.

I tucked it away in the closet behind some of my soccer stuff and went upstairs to get ready for bed.

I wish I could say that I played with it after that, but I never did. And when I moved out for college and was rifling through my stuff, I came across it again.

I put it up for free on Craigslist. I just left it by our front door and put 'free, you haul' and by the end of the day someone had picked it up.

Sometimes I wonder if the person who picked it up had anything wild happen to them. Was Mickey attached to the board and he was a package deal for the new owner? I'll never know. But what I do know is whenever I see anyone post about how fun playing with a Ouija board is, I make sure to comment and tell them how wrong they are. I don't get into my experiences; I just say they are evil. From my experience they are.

SHAKEN

I have had a number of instances when I used a Ouija board. After a while you come to understand that not every session will result in the contact with a spiritual entity. In most instances, very little is given. The one thing someone who has to keep in mind is to be respectful of the spirit(s) they are communicating with. In taunting them, you risk the invitation of evil energies. This is one such occasion when this happened to me.

One of my friends had recently lost her grandmother and was interested in using a Ouija board to try and contact her. I had told her there is no guarantee that we would be able to do so, but I'd be willing to try. I instructed her to bring an item that would be of personal importance to her loved one and we would try using it to draw the spirit to us.

On the night we agreed to meet, my friend showed up with her new boyfriend. To put it lightly the man was a skeptic. He didn't believe what we were doing was real and had tagged along in order to prove that his beliefs were correct. I had my reservations on allowing him to participate, but not wanting to offend my friend I kept those to myself.

In preparation for the session I had already set up the board in my office. I directed them all to some chairs I had arranged in a circle around it and told them to sit. My friend had brought her grandmother's wedding ring to help with communication. I took it from her and placed it on the table.

When I directed all of us placed a hand on the planchette, her boyfriend let out a scoff. I knew this negative energy wasn't going to help draw someone my friend loved to us and told him to take this seriously. We moved the pointer around in a circle and I told the spirits we were opening ourselves to communication with them. I then stated we were particularly interested in talking with her grandmother.

We continued to sit there waiting for something to step forward, but the planchette didn't move. The longer we waited, the larger the smirk got on the boyfriend's face. I tried three more times, imploring the spirits around us we were there to listen to them if they had something to say. Still, nothing.

That is when the boyfriend started laughing and stating that this whole thing was a fraud, me especially so. He told his girlfriend that she was stupid for believing in such things. That is when all of us heard an audible click then the lights went off. At first, I thought that there had been a power surge, but after looking at the switch on the wall, I could see it was in the off position.

I looked over to my friend and I could see her face was flushed. Sweat was pouring down her face, but she complained of being extremely cold. I looked at her boyfriend, he didn't seem to have anything wrong with him, but a look of terror was all over his face. Suddenly her eyes rolled in the back of her head, and she began having what looked like a seizure.

I ran over to her, she continued to convulse, her body jackknifing back and forth violently. The two of us tried to keep her still, but she was overpowering both of us. This continued on for almost 30 seconds before she finally went still.

Her eyes opened slowly, and she groaned in pain. Both of us helped her to her feet and set her back on the chair. I could still feel her burning up, and her entire body was slick with sweat. Her boyfriend was looking at me, but he didn't ask the questions I'm sure he was thinking. The truth was, I'd never seen anyone react like that while using a Ouija board before.

After a few minutes she found her voice. She asked her boyfriend to take her home. The two of us walked her out to their car and I got her situated in the passenger seat. I told them both I was sorry and didn't know what happened. I was almost positive it was the outburst by the boyfriend that had caused the whole thing, but it didn't seem the time to start pointing fingers.

Twenty minutes later, she called me weeping on the phone. She was telling me how sorry she was for the way her boyfriend had acted and knew it wasn't my fault and she didn't blame me. My friend said she felt like whatever had gotten inside of her had only left once they got home.

I firmly believe that Ouija boards aren't inherently evil. They are simply a tool one can use; it is the manner in which you use it that causes the problem. Spirits, like people, deserve your respect. If you give that to them, they will in return. If you treat them poorly, there can be a price to pay.

PROJECTILE

One year for Halloween I had decided to attend
a party with a few of my friends. We stayed late
into the night and were about ready to leave
when the guy who's house it was asked us if we
wanted to try out a Ouija board. It was getting
late, but none of us were really tired yet and it at
least gave us something to do other than drive
around trying to figure out what the plan for the
rest of the night would be

Craig led us into down a dark hallway to a door
that opened into what I could only assume was
some sort of office or study. Two walls had
built in shelves that were crammed full of
books. Most of them looked recent but some of

the titles appeared older and I ones I didn't recognize. There were a few chairs stationed around the room and in the center was a large square coffee table. A Ouija board and planchette had been placed on top of it.

The board was made of wood. The markings on top of it were intricate in design and appeared hand painted. The planchette was also made of wood with a clear glass lens that would serve as the indicator. From the patina, I assumed it was an antique and likely cost a great deal.

He told us all to grab a chair so we could sit around the table. For being someone in high school, it was obvious this particular board wasn't his and we'd probably not be doing this if his parents were here. A part of me felt guilty for being in here but now that we were, I was looking forward to seeing what was going to happen.

A small lamp that was in the corner of the room was the only source of light, but it gave us enough to see what the planchette would be pointing at. The five of us all place a hand on the device and swirled it in a circle while chanting the word Ouija five times. My heart fluttered a bit in my chest, a mix of excitement and apprehension.

"We are reaching out to any spirit that wants to contact us." Craig said. "Is there someone here?"

We all sat there, waiting for a message to come through. As the seconds ticked by all of us held are collective breath. Five, ten, fifteen seconds went by, yet nothing happened. I stared at the planchette, wanting it to move, yet afraid of what it might mean if it did.

"Should we ask again?" Tiffany asked. Her question was met by a couple of the others shushing her into silence. I was still looking at her when I felt the pointer begin to slide across the board. Ten eyes turned to watch what was being said.

The glass disk passed over the two rows of letters and then the numbers to settle itself over the word YES. I knew it hadn't moved the planchette, but that didn't mean one of the others didn't. Even though I questioned what had just happened, there was a heaviness in the air that hadn't existed a moment before.

Over the next few minutes different people took turns trying to figure out who this spirit was, when and how they died, anything they could think of to try and familiarize themselves with who this entity was. The letters T-O-M-A-S were given to us for a name, which we took to be the name Thomas. Every time someone asked for personal details other than the name, we would get a random jumble of letters and numbers that didn't make any sense.

The others, excited by the prospect of asking things about themselves started peppering the spirit with questions. Even before one person had been answered someone else would pipe in with their own. The others were starting to get testy with one another, wanting to get their questions answered.

We weren't the only ones that appeared to be getting frustrated though. The planchette started pointing to the word NO after a while no matter what question we asked. It didn't stop the others from continuing to ask the spirit things like, "Who is the guy I'll marry?" or "What is the perfect job for me?".

That is when things took a turn for the worst. Craig was in the middle of asking his latest query when I felt what seemed like a hand grasp my shoulder. It was cold, enough so that a burning sensation spread through my neck and down my arm. A gasp escaped me and then the planchette felt as though it was ripped from my hands and embedded itself into the wall three feet from the floor.

My friend Alexandra didn't wait long before she sprung to her feet and ran out of the room screaming. The rest of us stat there and just staring. My logical mind tried to come up with some explanation to what had just happened, but nothing seemed to make sense.

The planchette fell to the floor with a loud {crack}. The noise seemed to snap us all of us out of the stupor we were in. Where the pointer had hit, there was a hole about the size of a quarter in the drywall. I think we all counted ourselves lucky that none of us had been hit by it.

Craig walked over and picked it up and looked it over before returning the planchette to the tabletop. I really had no interest in touching it again, but I've always been told that you have to dismiss whatever spirit you have contacted, otherwise you risk it staying. Even though Alex wasn't there, we quickly moved the pointer to GOODBYE and pulled our hands away.

The experience has made me more cautious around things like Ouija boards. I've gone back to the house since then, and although I never saw anything, I swear the heaviness still seems to linger on.

POP-UPS

It seemed whenever my friends and I got together the conversations seemed to drift towards the supernatural. It shouldn't have been surprising since most of what we did together was watch scary movies and online videos. None of us really had any interest in doing any of these things ourselves, but the collective shutter we shared was something all of us enjoyed.

One evening my parents had brought up the subject of Ouija boards at dinner. They, being children of the 70's told us that both of them had used one in the past with some surprising success. Both of them shared stories in which they had come into contact with *something* that appeared to be a spirit. I distinctly remember telling them that they were so old, they couldn't use telephones to call their friends anymore, but rather a Ouija board. The joke got a chuckle from my dad and sister, but my mom just glared at me.

Despite my poor attempt at humor a seed had been planted in my mind. If there was any truth to what my parents had said, I would be willing to try using one for myself. The house we lived in was older, and I was sure there must be some spirits around from the previous owners. All I needed to do was pick up the board.

The opportunity arose about a week later when I went with my mom to our local big box store. I had nearly forgotten about it when I happened by a display on one isle that had a few board games sitting on it. Near the bottom sat a plain looking gold and red box that had the words Ouija Board printed on it. I grabbed one and asked my mom if we could get it. Initially it seemed as if she would deny my request, but after I gave her my best "Please." she relented.

As soon as the box hit the bottom of the cart, I had my cellphone out and had invited both of my friends over that night to try it out. The seemed just as excited as I was to finally do something that would bring us in direct contact to the ghosts and spirits, we were so interested in.

Just to add to the suspense of the moment, the three of us had to wait until the following evening. My mom told us that our ghost hunting adventures could wait for a night when we didn't have school the next day. Frankly I was convinced that it was of the greatest importance that we contacted our friends on the other side as soon as we could, but mom is the boss.

The next day seemed to drag on forever, but once the final bell rang the three of us beelined for my house. Pizza and videogames soon followed until the sun had set and we determined it was dark enough to attempt to communicate with any spirit that would be willing to talk. Now that I'm older, I'm not sure why it would matter what time of day it was for us to begin, but I think Hollywood has convinced a lot of people that spirits are only active at night.

We pulled the curtains shut and lit the two

candles that we could find in the house (sadly they were vanilla scented). Right before we began, I found myself looking at the board sitting on the floor of my bedroom. The idea that we could communicate with spirits using a board that had been mass produced out of cardboard with a planchette made of plastic seemed a bit naive. Even so, I think all of us still held a bit of trepidation in what we were attempting to do that evening.

Not wanting to be seen as a chicken I was the first to place my hands on the device and looked up at my friends in a silent challenge for them to follow suit. They seemed to get the hint and settled themselves down around the board and placed their hands on the planchette as well.

I started off by saying hello to any spirits who happened to be there with us and asked them if there was anyone present. Unfortunately, the pointer didn't seem interested in moving. I'd only asked one question and I was already doubting the validity of the board. Undeterred though I asked again. This time though the planchette slowly slid to the word YES.

I would like to tell you that I was absolutely

convinced we were speaking with a spirit, but the logical part of my mind was convinced one of my friends had been behind the message. I met each of their eyes in turn. Both of them gave me a silent shake of their head even though there was an excited grin on their faces. If I was to believe what they were telling me, we were in contact with a genuine ghost.

We continued to ask questions like what the spirit's name was, when and how s/he died, if they lived in this house. Basically, everything we could think of to establish an identity to look up later. Then one of my friends did something I later learned was a bad move. He asked the spirit for a sign that they were really there.

The reason this is a bad idea is, based on what some believe, it is giving the entity access to the physical plane through a door you are opening for it. After he demanded sign from the spirit the planchette spelled the letters PC. I had a laptop in my room, but I had closed the screen once we began to cut out any glow it would give off. Fortunately, there were no knocking noises, feelings of being touched, or any other physical manifestations that would indicate that the spirit had been allowed to cross over to this plane.

After that the planchette went frustratingly still. No matter what questions we asked, it refused to budge. It seemed our conversation was over. It was just as well since we were all interested in looking up the information that the spirit had given us to see if there was any truth to what was said.

As soon as I opened my laptop, the entire screen was covered in popup messages that ranged from advertisements to windows saying that I had a virus on my computer. All three of us sat there staring at the screen not sure what to believe. Was it possible that a ghost had messed with my computer? I had never heard of such a thing but there didn't seem to be any other explanation for it.

OPEN INVITATION

A few months ago I was spending some time with a few of my girlfriends. It had been quite a while since all of us had gotten together and it was nice to catch up on the comings and goings of our lives. Like most adults, the daily events of our lives hadn't changed much since our marriages. Sure, we had our gripes, but what couple doesn't?

As the evening progressed, we opened a few bottles of wine as we retold stories from the days when we had first met in college. It truly was just like old times. On a whim, I suggested that maybe we could try out the Ouija board that my teenage daughter had bought for a party a couple years back. I really thought it would turn into something for us all to laugh about, but in fact it was just the opposite.

Once the question was asked, all three of us got really quiet. It wasn't that I was scared to use the board itself, but rather I truly wanted to. The silence stretched on for a solid thirty seconds before Shannon said she would be willing to try it. Even though her words held some hesitancy in them, her eyes were smiling at the idea. Lori, always up for whatever agreed as well.

It took me a few minutes to locate, but I did manage to uncover the board. Because the three of us were true experts on setting up a location for a seance, we cleared off the kitchen table and placed a bunch of tea candles around the room. Frankly, when we started, I thought it more likely we get a visit from the fire department than a spirit.

In expert fashion, we all placed our hands on the planchette and waited as if we expected it to start all on its own. As you must know, proper Ouija board session always starts with a pause to read the directions that come with it.

As the owner of the board, I was the one selected to ask the questions once we let the spirits know we were there to listen to any messages they had. The first and most obvious question I started with was if there were any entities there with us. To my surprise, it didn't take long for the planchette to slide over to YES.

I looked up to my friends, a silent question being asked of both of them with my eyes. Both of them in unison shook their heads that they hadn't moved it. "Well, I didn't either." I told them.

I didn't put it past Lori or Shannon to play a prank like this so I asked the "spirit" who they were, your basic spirit Caller ID if you will. The pointer stayed right on top of the word YES. This told me one of two things, either we had a bashful ghost, or the name and number was unlisted.

"I guess we'll come back to that question later." I said which elicits a giggle from Lori.

Moving on, I asked the spirit if it had some sort of message that it wanted to deliver. The planchette started moving quickly from letter to letter, but nothing it spelled out made any sense. I was becoming more convinced that one of my friends was moving it or the spirit was illiterate.

I've about had it with this Ouija thing when I ask "What is it that you want? I don't understand what you're trying to tell us."

The pointer spells out the letters Y-O-U then stopped. Something about it didn't sit right. Even if my friends would have wanted to freak me out, which this had accomplished, it wasn't really their style. And if the spirit was in the house, it had to know it wouldn't work between the two of us. The whole dead/living thing didn't seem like a hurdle we could overcome.

If it was my friends, I wasn't about to let them get the last laugh. "Well, if you want me, then here I am."

The shocked look on my friends' faces was enough to know that I'd won this round. Really though the shock was from what I'd just said. The instructions on the board clearly said don't invite things into yourself or taunt the spirits when using the board. With my last statement I'd basically done both

I sat there waiting for something profound to happen, but the seconds ticked by, and nothing happened. There was no knock, no sounds, no apparitions. Not wanting to annoy the spirits, I suggested that we stop. Both Shannon and Lori agreed. We thanked the entity for joining us and started to move the planchette towards the word GOODBYE.

The spirit seemed to have other ideas though. I could feel the pointer being pushed in another direction. Curious as to what would happen next, I let it move as it willed which happened to be to the word NO. All of us looked at each other, a little stunned as to what we were witnessing. At this point I was almost positive that the three of us weren't moving the planchette.

In accepting this, my declaration to the entity

seemed foolish if not outright dangerous. I needed to know what I had invited in. "Who is this that we're speaking to?" Again, it pointed to the word NO on the board.

Fear and frustration fueled me repeating myself. This time I was nearly yelling the question. It only took three letters before I knew what it was spelling. D-E-M-O-N.

"Kristen, if you're doing this, it's not funny." Lori told me. I could see real fear in her eyes now. From the look on mine I'm sure she knew I was thinking the same thing. This had gotten beyond our control. As the one in charge of the questions, I yanked the planchette from their fingers and placed it over the word GOODBYE before throwing it across the room where it clattered to a halt next to the fridge.

I sat there staring at it. I don't know what I expected it to do, but thankfully it just sat there on the ground until I went over and picked it up. I went back to the table and picked up the box and board and took everything out to the trash. I didn't want that thing in my house.

I'd like to say that is where it ended, but that isn't the case. Since that night I have been plagued with horrible night terrors where I see people being torn apart. The only way I can guarantee a full night sleep is take a powerful sleep medication that knocks me out completely. Lori and Shannon thankfully don't seem to have suffered the same affliction. I assume this is because I was the one who taunted the spirit. Unfortunately, I had to learn this lesson the hard way. When you invite something in, you take the chance it isn't something good.

DEAR GRANDMA

Early on in my life I lost my mother to cancer. She had been raising me by herself and after much deliberation it was decided that my Grandmother Ruth would be the one to raise me. The two-generation gap could create issues at times, but there was no doubt the woman loved me as if I was her own child. She was there in the front row cheering me on during all my sporting events, recitals, and graduations. Other than the fact she didn't give birth to me, she was still my mom.

During my junior year in college I got a phone call from my aunt telling me my grandmother was in the hospital with pneumonia. The words "It's time to say goodbye" sent a shockwave through my heart. I couldn't believe the woman who had been there for so many of the most important events of my life was going to be gone.

I flew back to Georgia the two days later to spend the last days of her life at her bedside. We spent our time reliving the moments that were most meaningful to each other. The funny thing was, most of the most important times didn't involve the milestone events, but rather the simple things that I took for granted, the dinners we had together, trips to the park, her holding me when I cried after my first boyfriend, and I split up.

For two days we were able to share our memories with each other. On the third day she slipped into a coma and passed away. As hard as it was to see her gone, I was grateful for the time I had with her.

The funeral came a few days later and was a well-attended affair. Seeing all the faces of her friends and family showed me just how many people's lives she had touched and been a part of.

After everyone had left, I volunteered to help go

through her house and get things in order. There would be a number of things that had sentimental value to people, and I wanted to make sure they got them. Plus, it was a chance to spend time around the place that I'd called home during my childhood.

During the second day I was going through one of her closets when I came across a Ouija board. I'd never seen this type of thing before and was curious how it had gotten there. Grandma Ruth had always been a casual church going woman, attending on most major holidays and gatherings but had never mentioned any interest in the supernatural.

I had always been a big fan of the shows where groups are seeking out spirits. I'd never personally done anything myself, but seeing as I was in my grandmother's house, I figured it was possible I could contact her.

I picked her bedroom as the place where there would be the strongest connection to her. I sat down on her bed with the board in my lap and concentrated on a mental picture of Grandma Ruth. I didn't see her as she'd been in the casket, but the bright and vibrant woman that lived in my childhood memories.

Keeping my eyes closed I began to speak. "Grams, I'm here in your room. I just wanted to talk if you're here with me."

The planchette didn't move for a few seconds, but after a moment it started to slide in small jerking motions. I watched it spell out letters one by one. S-U-N-F-L-O-W-E-R it was the nickname that she had given me since I was a little girl. I started to cry; I couldn't help it. No one would know that name but her.

After that my words came out in a flood. I just kept going on and on about how I was going to miss her, and I didn't know what I was going to do without her there anymore. Just like when she was alive, she didn't say anything until I was done. It wasn't that I didn't have more to say to her, but the sobbing had overcome my ability to do so.

I sat there, my shoulders hitching up and down, as I cried on her bed. From nowhere I felt a hand rubbing circles on my back and I could distinctly smell my grandmother's perfume in the air. I was alone in the house, but I wasn't scared. I knew who this person was, and she'd never hurt me.

Finally I was able to find my voice. "Thanks Grams."

The planchette started moving around the board again. A-L-W-A-Y-S-T-H-E-R-E. It was a shorter version of what the last thing she'd told me in the hospital before she died. A new wave of tears started to fall, but this time they were happy ones.

When I told her goodbye on the board a sense of peace had come over me. When she told me on her deathbed that she'd always watch out for me, and she'd never truly be gone I thought she meant it as a way to reduce the pain of her death. instead, it was a promise that she'd kept.

Whenever I find there is some problem that I can't manage to work out, I'll talk to my grandmother and more often than not I get some sort of inspiration. I know she's there, and I know that I'll see her again when my time comes.

MISPLACED

A few months ago, I had gone over to a friend's house for a sleepover. The events that led up to it aren't really important but eventually we decided it would be fun to try out a Ouija board. All of us, not really knowing what we were actually dealing with all jumped at the chance to try it out. After all, what 14-year-old wouldn't want to see if there was a chance to talk with spirits?

We were all sitting in a circle with the board in the middle of us. Erica decides since it was her party that she would be the one to ask all of the questions which we'd written down on a piece of paper beforehand. We'd agreed that we would keep the questions innocent and stay away from things like "How will I die?" and the like. Even though I wasn't sure of how real this whole thing was, I just didn't think that asking such things was a good idea.

As soon as we started, the planchette began to move almost immediately when we asked if there was anyone that wanted to talk with us. The spirit identified itself as a boy named Trevor. He told us that he lived in the area during the late 1800's and had died of some sort of infection. He said that he was around our age when we asked his age.

We continued to ask him questions about himself, but he seemed to be more interested in learning about us. We told him what things we liked to do, what sports we were into, basically anything. He seemed nice and charming, and it felt easy to talk to him. I think that we should have taken it as a warning that he might not have been who he said he was when he would avoid any questions about himself, but we just were too excited to be communicating with Trevor to notice.

After about an hour he told us that he was getting tired and needed to go and rest. We told him goodbye, but not before he made us promise to come back and talk with him later.

For almost twenty minutes after the four of us talked about how much we liked Trevor. None of us seemed to think it was weird that he didn't talk about himself, in fact, one of my friends said she wished some of the boys we went to school with could take a hint from Trevor about just that thing.

It was nearly midnight when Erica brought out the Ouija board again and we asked Trevor if he was there. The planchette went immediately to YES. This time though the conversation was different. He seemed almost to be distant. When we asked him what was wrong, he told us that he was sad that we wouldn't be there to talk with him, that he'd be alone again once we left the next day.

I really didn't know what to say to that. I could understand wanting to have friends, but there didn't seem to be anything we could do to change that. We told him we'd come over now and again to talk with him using the Ouija board but that didn't seem to make things better. He told us that he was going to leave when Erica's face brightened with an idea.

She asked Trevor if he was limited to just her house or was, he capable of going with others. Later we would learn this is just what "he" was hoping for. He told us that he could, but someone would have to invite him into wherever he was going. Here should have been our second red flag from Trevor, but none of us really knew what we were doing.

It was a little bizarre thinking that we were there discussing whether or not we wanted a ghost living with us. In the end though all of us told Trevor that he was welcome to come visit us any time he wanted to, that we would be his friends. After we told him this, Trevor seemed to get excited and more talkative again until we told him around 1:30 that we needed to go to sleep.

The next morning was spent getting ready to go

back to my own house and we didn't make any time to use the Ouija board again. Really, I thought that it would be the last time I'd have to speak to Trevor. I was wrong though.

Over the next couple weeks things started to get a little strange, and not just around my house, but in all of ours. It started with hearing light footsteps all hours of the night, but when I'd go look nobody would be there. I always felt like I was being watched, especially when one of the girls that had been there that night were there. In the back of my mind, I kept thinking it was Trevor, but I didn't really want to believe that was true.

One night the four of us got together to confront Trevor about his behavior, but he denied that it was him. He told us he wouldn't ever do such a thing to his friends. Frankly though, none of us believed him.

After that night it went from noises to things being moved. To this day, some of the things he took I have yet to locate. I think we might have upset him by calling him out like we did.

Really, I'm not sure at this point if Trevor is actually the spirit of a boy or something else. I've never gotten the feeling he means us any harm, but more that he is mischievous and likes to play.

After doing some research online, I figured out that he had told us the truth when he said that we had to invite him in. Now I don't know if were stuck with Trevor or if there is a way to rid ourselves of this pesky spirit. We are going to try and give him a choice, but I fear that we may have to force him to go.

SCRATCHES

When it came to things that most people would consider paranormal or supernatural, I always thought that I was more open minded than most. I'd gone on a number of investigations around the country and had collect some pretty compelling evidence that would lead me to believe that there is something after this existence we all call life. In doing so I always was told I needed to take precautions when dealing with entities that are not part of the physical realm.

In my house I'd collect various crystals and

symbols of power that were supposed to shield me from negative entities and the like. This practice came about after a particularly frightening experience I had while using a Ouija board. This is that story.

I was just out of college when me and my girlfriend at the time were walking through an antique store when she happened to spot something on a shelf. At first I thought it was a strangely decorated box, but when she opened it up and I saw a planchette sitting inside a velvet lined impression I clearly saw it for what it was, an old Ouija board.

Even at that age I had more than a passing interest in the paranormal and I begged her to let me buy it thinking she'd want it for herself. I stuck out my lip in an exaggerated pout and batted my lashes while letting out what I hoped was a pathetic "Please...". I'd used this tactic before too much success and this time was no different. She relented and I was the one who ended up with the antique.

That evening I went about cleaning the dust off

and polishing the wood. My initial intention was this would be a decoration rather than something I'd actually use. Because of its age and condition, which was very good, I didn't want to risk it being damaged. Still, it seemed a shame to just set it aside without using it at least once.

They say it isn't always a good idea to use a board by yourself, but I was the only one home at the time and even if that hadn't been the case, no one I lived with was likely to want to join me, either from fear or disbelief. So, I sat down on the floor in my study and stated that I was there to receive any messages that the spirits would like to communicate to me.

Only seconds had passed before the planchette started to move slowly across the board. It spelled the word H-E-L-L-O after which I returned the greeting. I asked if the spirit would tell me its name, but it quickly went to the word NO. This wasn't the first time I'd dealt with a spirit that didn't want to tell me its name, but there had been times in the past when a negative energy had come through with the same thing occurring.

I continued to ask questions to which the entity seemed to be giving very vague answers. When I confronted it on this very fact the spirit seemed to get extremely upset. It began using offensive language and the planchette would move in quick jerking motions.

At this point I was sure that I was dealing with some sort of malevolent spirit or demonic entity. I knew from my readings into these beings that their name is something that holds power over them, so I asked again what its name was. Again, I received an answer of NO. The pointer began moving in large angry circles over the board at such a high rate that I had to focus to keep my hands in contact with it.

I knew that I needed to end the session. I went to move the planchette to GOODBYE, but in doing so I felt three streaks of pain lance down my back. I yelped in pain and momentarily forgot about the Ouija board on my lap.

My back felt like it was on fire, but I was finally

able to move the pointer to where it hovered over GOODBYE. As I did so the pain seemed to reduce immensely, although it didn't disappear altogether.

All thought and care for the Ouija board gone, I threw it off me and ran to the bathroom. Even before I lifted my shirt, I saw three red lines running up my shirt where I had bled into the fabric. When I lifted my shirt, the sight was even worse. Not only was I bleeding, but the scratches were an angry red. small blisters were beginning to form along the jagged lines.

It was obvious that the negative spirit had attacked me when I tried to learn its identity. I knew I'd opened myself up to the attack by not shielding myself from the negative spirit when I began. In most cases I would have said some sort of prayer so only benevolent spirits would come through, but in my haste to try out my new purchase I'd not done so.

Like any tool, the Ouija board is not good nor evil. I made the mistake of not doing what I had to so I would be protected. I still possess the board and it sits in a prominent location in my house. Now it serves as a decoration though, rather than a medium to contact the spiritual realm. I don't expect that to change any time soon.

DANCING SHADOWS

I had an opportunity a little while ago to take part in a group investigation of an old sanitarium. Me and about twenty other amateur ghost hunters signed up to take part in the experience in hopes of catching some video footage, EVP's or other evidence proving the existence of the supernatural.

I didn't have much as far as equipment was concerned but at the time, I had a decent recorder and I decided to take a Ouija board with me. I figured using them in tandem would give me a chance to compare the audio I captured with the messages I received on the board.

I should have known I was in over my head when I got the first look at the building. Dirt and grime covered the entirety of the two-story building from decades of neglect. The plants that had survived had taken over what once was the entry to the grounds. Nature was in the process of taking back what was once hers.

The bus stopped outside the front gate where two people stood with bright smiles on their faces. I suppose they could have really loved their jobs, but someone who looked forward to a place such as this has something wrong with them.

All of us disembarked from the shuttle and we were gathered together for a brief safety briefing concerning the sanitarium. We were told the right-hand side of the upper floor was off limits because they couldn't guarantee that the floor would hold our weight. They also paired us off with a partner in case something happened somebody was there to help them.

We all told them we understood what was expected and then, those like me who came alone were paired with other ghost hunters. My partner was a woman in her late 40's named Diane. To my chagrin she informed me that this was her first time doing something like this, but she'd watched a lot of television where people had so she was sure she could handle it. Frankly I had my doubts.

Every group was given a pair of flashlights along with a map of the layout of the place which was labeled with the areas where most of the reported activity had been witnessed. I quickly scanned the piece of paper and made a mental note to check out the morgue and the lockdown units. I was here to communicate with a spirit, and I figured that there wasn't any place more likely for that to happen than these locations. I just hoped Diane was up for the challenge, if not though I'd go by myself.

We made our way across the fifty yards to the front door and we made our way into the entry room of the building. Other than the dirt and debris on the floor, it looked like any other hospital. Back when this place was open, I can only imagine the contrast between this room and what lay beyond for those who called this place home.

Diane had kept the map for us, and I asked her where she wanted to start. To my surprise she told me that the morgue was the first place she thought we should go. I agreed with her, and we took off towards the stairwell that led down to that part of the building. I would have thought we wouldn't be the only ones to go, but it seemed the others were willing to ease their way into the evening rather than jump right into it.

On our way down we had a chance to make a bit of a game plan. She had brought a handheld video camera and an audio recorder similar to mine. I suggested that we use the Ouija board and set up the video camera and recorders to see if we could capture anything. She agreed, but I could tell she was a little scared at the prospect of what might happen. It is one thing to say you're up to go to a place like this, it's another to stare that fear in the face.

The basement smelled like I thought it would, stale air and mildew. The beams of the flashlights illuminated the peeling white paint on concrete walls. A single hallway T'd left and right. According to the map, the morgue was at the end of the hall on the left.

The ceiling was low, and it felt like it was pressing down on top of me. I had the urge to duck down to keep from hitting my head even though there was at least a foot of clearance. Our footsteps echoed loudly in both directions making seem as if we were being followed by someone just outside our cocoon of light. I knew this was going to be a bit unnerving down here, but what I was feeling far exceeded my expectations.

On our way down the hall, small doorways were inset into the wall. Not all of them had doors which let us quickly inspect them. From what we guessed they might have been alcoves for storage in years past, but now they laid empty. At the end of the hall an opening came into view, the metal door had been left ajar leaving a patch of darkness.

To my surprise the door opened soundlessly when I pushed it open. The room had three concrete islands about waist high in the center with large holes in the floor that at one time served as drains. I tasted bile in the back of my throat as I thought about what vile substances had been washed down those holes.

Diane began by setting up her camera in one corner of the room where it would be able to capture as wide of an angle as possible. I put out the Ouija board and recorders on the center slab and positioned one of the flashlights so we would be able to see what letters the planchette pointed to.

We moved the planchette in a circle and stated that we were willing to listen to any messages the spirits had. After we completed the opening, it felt like the temperature in the room dropped almost instantly. I'd heard of cold spots before but experiencing one firsthand was unsettling.

The flashlight appeared to flicker and the planchette began to glide slowly across the board. The letters came slowly at first, but by the fourth or fifth letter, the spirit seemed to get a handle on the device. W-H-O-Y-O-U it spelled to which Diane, and I introduced ourselves. We asked the spirit their name was, but the letters S-C-R-E-D were given which we took to mean the spirit was afraid to tell us.

We continued to ask questions of the spirit but the answers we got either didn't make sense or the planchette didn't move. I was starting to think this wasn't going anywhere when something hit the door behind us. The loud metallic bang had caused both Diane and I to jump. We returned our hands to the planchette and asked the spirit if that was him/her that had made the noise. The pointer quickly moved to the word NO.

"Then who did it?" I asked.

The planchette gave us four letters. T-H-E-M. Every hair on my body felt like it was standing on end. I looked around but the flashlight did little to dispel the shadows in the room. I'd seen enough of this room for me to know that we needed to leave. From the look on her face, it appeared Diane agreed with me.

The two of us moved the planchette over to the word GOODBYE and I said that we were closing the session and we were leaving the spirits here in peace. The two of us quickly packed up our gear and walked quickly out of the morgue, down the hall and up the stairs to the first floor of the building. The entire time we were leaving it felt to me like something was either following us or watching us leave. The echo of our footsteps did little to assure me that this wasn't the case.

Finally back on what I considered safe ground Diane and I were anxious to see what the camera and recorders had caught.

We started by replaying my audio recording. You could clearly hear my voice as I went about asking questions. It wasn't until I got to the part when I asked who made the banging noise a light whisper could be heard saying "Bad Men".

I know Diane had heard it to because we both looked right at each other. I never expected to capture such a clear EVP. When we listened to Diane's recorder the voice could not be heard. I think both of us were a little disappointed at this because it would have meant corroborating evidence that it hadn't been an anomaly.

The real exciting thing though was when we reviewed the footage caught on the video camera. She had set it to low light mode which gave us a better view. The camera had been pointing towards the doorway and when the banging happened, I barely even registered it. My mouth was already hanging open from what I'd seen. Right next to the door, there appeared to be two humanoid shaped figures.

We both conferred with each other about the positioning of the lights and the possibility that it was us creating the shadows but based on the angles it wasn't possible for us to be casting them. Was this the "Bad Men" our spirit had talked about or was this the spirit that was speaking with us?

That night in the morgue was an exciting and terrifying experience. It gave me a firsthand look into the supernatural realm and a better respect for it. Places like that sanitarium are the types of locations where spirits continue on, forgotten, a continuation of the lives they lived.

ORIGINS
A HORROR NOVEL
COMING 2022

ORIGINS
PROLOGUE

Detective Robert Jones watched as the firemen tried to put out the blaze. The air was thick with black smoke, scorching the edges of the building with crippling red burns. The windows had shattered, raining shards of glass onto the hotel's front plaza, more flames licking through the jagged edges with burning ferocity. The screams had gone quiet a few moments ago. Only the hungry growl and crackle of the flames remained, silencing the cries of those still trapped inside the hotel. Now, the firemen wielded industrial-duty hoses against the raging inferno. The onslaught of water was doing little to quell the fire …

Jones knew it was unlikely anyone had survived. The fire was too intense, too vicious. Nobody was able to get in or out without being consumed by those ravenous flames. Not even the firefighters dispatched to the scene had enough protective equipment to get inside safely.

Beyond the smell of smoke and ash, Jones was certain he could pick up something else; something faintly fragrant and acrid, like the smell of burning flesh or singed hair. He tried not to think about it too much—not when there was so little that he could have done. The firemen had been dispatched as soon as the call came in, but even by then, it was already too late. The fire had already claimed its victims.

"Look at this," Detective Rachel Burke said, drawing his attention away from the blaze. She was kneeling beside a body on the ground, her head cocked as she peered closely at the victim's face. "Look around her mouth."

Jones cleared his throat of smoke and glanced down at the woman sprawled out beside the fountain. The grand feature had been turned off, and the water that pooled at the bottom was cloudy with ash and fallen debris. Somehow, all the luxury and grandeur seemed superfluous against the disaster ongoing around them. The fire, tearing through the hotel without a care for the money and pride that had been thrown into it. Ripped apart in a matter of minutes.

The woman at his feet was young, perhaps mid- to late-twenties, clad in a long gold dress and heels. Her hair was done up in tight blond ringlets and her left arm was thrown out beside her, her fingers reaching toward an empty mug that had somehow survived the fall and remained intact. There were other bodies scattered around the plaza, but they had been victims of the fire, their bodies almost burned to burned beyond recognition? This woman was the only one who seemed to have been killed before the flames reached her.

Her eyes were still open, once a bright blue it seemed, but now clouded over with the veneer of death. Her skin had gone clammy and gray, and Jones thought that something about her seemed almost uncannily vacant, as though she wasn't quite dead, but a puppet waiting for its master.

At his partner's instruction, Jones leaned down to inspect the woman's mouth. Her lips were painted a bright rouge, but they had slackened in death and he could see the foam seeping up between them, as well as the strange discoloration at the corners of her mouth.

"What do you think it is?" he asked, wrinkling his nose at the smell wafting up from her. She couldn't have been dead long, but the throes of decay were already setting in.

Burke's thin eyebrows shot up as she pointed to the victim's mouth, her gloved finger prodding the corner of her lips. "Looks like poisoning to me. See that residue around her mouth? That's common in poison victims," she said, flicking a glance toward the scotch glass. A thin line of red lipstick was smeared around the rim. "We'll have the contents of her drink analyzed. It seems the most likely culprit in administering the poison."

Jones nodded ruminatively. Burke always had an eye for evidence. "What do you think happened here? There's a lot going on, but nobody seems to have any answers." They'd questioned a few witnesses who had managed to escape the fire, but most had no idea what had happened and hadn't seen anyone suspicious in the moments before. It was yet unclear whether it was an accident, or a coordinated attack. All they could do for the moment was use what evidence they had and wait until the hotel was deemed safe to search.

Although, it was likely the fire had destroyed any evidence that might have been left inside.

Burke shook her head, pursing her lips. "I can't really say. With the fire and the poison, it seems a lot more happened here than you'd originally think. What about you? Do you have any ideas?"

Detective Jones looked up from the body to the inferno blazing through the hotel. The flames licking the corners of the building seemed somehow alive, and he could feel the hunger and the anger emanating from them. "I can't explain it, but … I don't like the feel of this place."

"How do you mean?"

Jones shifted his feet, lifting a gloved finger to his chin. "I'm not the superstitious type or anything, but something about the place just feels wrong to me. Like all this glamour and luxury is just a façade. It's almost … like this place is cursed."

Burke stared at him in incredulous silence for a minute, before barking out a laugh. "Cursed? Really, Jones?"

The detective shook his head, waving off her apparent amusement. "Yeah, yeah, maybe this heat is making me delirious," he muttered.

Burke sobered. "Maybe. Let's move away from the fire and get someone to collect the body."

Jones nodded in silence as Burke wandered off to find the paramedics, but he stayed where he was, casting an eye over the place.

Despite the humidity of the air against his skin from the fire, a chill touched the back of his neck, running all the way down his spine. Something akin to unease stirred in his chest. The recorded number of accidents that had happened at this hotel couldn't be mere coincidence. Maybe *cursed* wasn't as far off as he'd thought.

Shaking it off, he turned and followed Burke.

ORIGINS
CHAPTER 1

Thomas Hartley tried to be a good husband. He really did.

From the moment he had met Rose, he'd whisked her off her feet and done everything she had wanted, given her everything she had asked for. He had given her the ultimate dream, what she had always desired: a hotel. A place where they could live in solitude in a beautiful building of their own making, earning enough to be comfortable and more.

He'd had the hotel built from scratch, all according to her design plans, the way she had envisioned it for all those years of dreaming.

She chose the rooms, the carpets, the furnishings and fixtures, every single painting and sculpture that set the place apart as a high-class luxury. He had sat back and let her do it all, let her thrive in the creative process, making all the decisions. He never said a word of disagreement, never showed his scruples. Never admitted how much he truly detested her taste. But he'd been a good husband. He'd done everything he could to make Rose aware of that fact; to make sure she knew she was one of the lucky ones. The ones who had husbands that would do anything for them. She never had to worry about anything because he would always be there to sort things out when they went wrong. All she had to do was have fun.

Well, now it was his turn.

He wanted to have some fun too.

He'd been a good husband, but now he wanted to play.

Thomas had been what his parents called a "troubled kid."

He'd never been very good at making friends, despite his interest in other children. He was intelligent for his age too, more observant and perceptive than the other kids. Because of that, he'd been a rather lonely child. A lonely child who coveted attention.

He spent a lot of time on his own, out in the woods behind his house.

It was there he had his first brush with death.

He'd been playing among the trees, chasing bugs with a sharpened stick, when he stumbled over something that made a wet, cracking noise when he hit it with his foot. When he peered down, he saw the remains of a fox carcass, half-rotted among the weeds and thistles at his feet. When he'd stepped in it, some of the blood and viscera had leaked out onto his shoe, staining it a gruesome red.

Struck with disgust and a budding curiosity, he used his stick to scrape the mess off his shoe, then used the pointed edge to move some of the fox's loose skin out of the way, exposing its insides. The smell had been rancid, the sight of the organs and the bones gruesome to a child's mind, but it had sparked something in him—some kind of excitement, a curiosity about life and death. Questions about biology and animal physiology plagued him; the way the body worked, ideas of death and mortality.

Death became a fascination for him.

After his encounter with the fox in the woods, his curiosity only grew. He began to purposely go out into the woods in search of more dead things, whether they were fresh or old, the blood still wet and bright or dried to a dark, crusty brown. It didn't matter. The process of decay was a natural part of death, after all.

He played around with death throughout his childhood, his own secret occupation. Nobody else could know the joys of poking, stabbing, dissecting those pitiful little creatures out in the woods. And when he found no more dead ones, he made them himself. He would set traps full of pointy metal teeth and wait for the prey to stumble in them unawares, watching them thrash and squirm helplessly as the teeth bit into them and made them bleed. He was always watching, from the shadows of the trees; watching their struggles grow still, their eyes turn dark and cloudy, their screams dying in their throats. No animal was quite the same. Some of them fought to the very end. Others accepted their fate and succumbed to death quietly. Then they would be his to play with.

Those woods behind his childhood home held a lot of his secrets. All those bones buried deep beneath the soil, his handiwork.

Of course, he'd had to grow up at some point. And as he got older, things changed.

Into early adulthood, he was plagued with voices. Those sinister little whispers in his head, filling his mind with morbid fantasies. Reminding him of the pleasure he'd gotten out in those woods, telling him he needed more, deserved more.

Animals weren't enough anymore. He needed bigger prey. Bigger toys to play with.

So he'd waited. Bided his time. Waiting for the perfect opportunity. All the while, those voices continued to taunt him, to haunt him in the night with fantasies of blood and death, memories of his childhood, when nobody had understood him, when his parents had condemned him for being wrong, for being broken. Disillusioned with life, he'd spent many years learning that people like him didn't have a place amongst normal society. He was an outcast, a reject. But he wanted that to change. He tried to suppress his desires, but that didn't work. Instead, he learned to hide them. He did everything he could to appear *normal*. He was still intelligent, still capable, and it wasn't long before he got a well-paying job and began to integrate properly into the social settings he had been exempt from in his younger years.

And then he met Rose. Naïve little Rose, who had fallen under his spell. He gave her everything she wanted. He gave her the seclusion, the privacy, the luxury that she craved. And in return, he gained her trust, her passion, her desire. And those hidden obsessions began to creep back in, looking for a new outlet. When Rose had proposed building a hotel, in some remote, far-off valley, it had seemed perfect. Everything had aligned as he had desired. He would have the perfect opportunity to satisfy his own cravings, and the perfect façade to hide behind. A future of blood and death, just as he had always wanted.

He'd been a good husband to her. He'd sacrificed years to get to where he was now.

But now it wasn't enough. He was finished with the lies, with the preparation. Now, he was ready.

He wanted more. Needed more. More screams, more blood, more suffering.

He wanted to kill. Dreams and memories weren't enough anymore. He had a craving for blood, for death, and his wife's dream hotel would become the site of his dream, too.

After all, who would miss a lonely traveler, all the way out here?

ORIGINS

CHAPTER 2

Thomas leaned forward slightly over the counter, bridging his fingers together as he flashed a dazzling grin at the young woman standing opposite him. "Your name?" he asked, his voice like silk.

He'd gotten far better at charming people since his lonely childhood years. He'd learned how to attract, to beguile and allure, to throw people off his scent with a smile and a wink, so that they might never suspect the darkness hiding beneath, the fascination with death that he had harbored since he was only a boy.

"Oh, it's Susan Livowitz," she answered in a low southern drawl, shifting her suitcase from one hand to the other as she peered up at him from beneath her lashes.

"Ahh, such a beautiful name," Thomas cooed, his grin widening. In the bright fluorescents above him, his eyes gleamed like emeralds. "Susan…"

With a gloved hand, she tucked a strand of honey hair behind her ear, smiling sheepishly at him. "Thank you."

"How long are you staying?"

"Just a few days."

"I see. Not long at all." Thomas reached behind him and plucked a key from the wall. "I'll put you in Room Five. Is that satisfactory?"

"Yes, that's perfect, thank you," she said, taking the key from him. He reached forward a little more than he needed to, making sure his fingers brushed hers for a fleeting second. Her skin was soft and warm, sending a faint tingle through him.

"Allow me to carry your luggage," he said, stepping out from behind the desk with a slight bow, another charming smile. Appearances were everything in places like these.

"Oh, there's really no need, I can—"

"Please, I insist," he interrupted, taking the bag from her before she could protest further. Now that he was closer, he could smell her perfume, light and fruity, and he dug his teeth into his lip.

His mind was swirling with dangerous thoughts. Uncontrolled desires. He couldn't let her read them on his face.

"Thank you," Susan said, a faint blush appearing on her cheeks.

She's a shy one, he thought as he led the way to her room. *I wonder if she screams with that southern drawl. Or if she's a quiet one. I wonder if her blood is as red as those pouty lips ...*

He schooled his features into a tight smile as she came to walk beside him, running a finger through her hair nervously.

"Are you new to the area?" he asked, keeping his tone polite.

"Yes, I've never been here before. It's rather out of the way. But it's a lovely place."

"Indeed. My wife likes the seclusion of it," he said offhandedly.

"Y-your wife?"

He chuckled lightly, noticing the surprise on her face before she sobered. "Yes, she's the one who runs this place, really."

"I see."

"Although, I hardly see her these days. She's always so busy," he continued with a wink. "It's up to me to entertain our guests."

Another hesitant smile appeared on her lips. Thomas hid a smirk. He would definitely enjoy playing with this one.

"Well, here we are. Room five. Please ring the service bell if you require any further assistance."

"Thank you, sir."

He grinned. "Please, call me Thomas."

"Oh, then, thank you, Thomas."

"Enjoy your stay."

She unlocked the door to her room, casting a furtive glance over her shoulder before dragging her suitcase inside and shutting it behind her.

Thomas's smirk returned, and a tingle of excitement thrummed through his veins like an ember sparkling to life.

She was the one. His next target. She was perfect. Quiet and feminine, not overly confident or brash. Easy to manipulate. The perfect toy.

He would have fun with her, he knew it.

Thomas walked back to the front desk, savoring the excitement he was feeling. His fingers were still hot from the touch of her skin, and he already anticipated what it would be like to feel her bones snap beneath them, her blood spilling over her creamy skin. This was what he had been waiting for. A hotel full of potential suspects, a distraught hotel owner. It was the perfect scenario for him to satisfy his desires without getting caught with blood on his hands.

This wasn't the woods anymore, where he had to hide under the shade of the trees, scavenging for dead things to play with. This was the real world. Full of living puppets.

And it was all his for the taking.

ORIGINS
CHAPTER 3

Rose stood unmoving, her hip resting gently against the chair by the window as she stared straight ahead. Despite the blank look she tried to hold, her thoughts were swirling through her mind.

It had been two weeks since she should have bled. She'd never gone this long before without bleeding, and the consequences were pulling a tight string around her stomach.

Was she pregnant? It was the only possible reason, wasn't it?

"Can you hold still, ma'am?"

A voice drew her out of her thoughts, and she realized she'd let a crack show in her expression. The paint peeked his head over the top of the canvas, a scowl shadowing his brows.

She quickly fixed her expression and straightened, and he dipped back behind it, his paintbrush flicking idly.

Rose fought the urge to roll her eyes. How long did they expect her to stand here, completely still?

Thomas was sitting in the chair next to her, posing with his chin in the air. At least he didn't have to stand the whole time. Rose's ankles were beginning to ache and she struggled to keep her shoulders straight against the urge to slouch.

The portrait had been his idea, of course. He'd been eager to get it completed as soon as possible so that they could hang it over their bed, as though their life was some kind of trophy romance, for everyone to sec and admire.

But Rose knew that wasn't the case at all. The reality of their marriage at the moment was far from perfect. She'd noticed that Thomas had become more and more withdrawn over the past few weeks, seemingly without cause. It felt like as each day passed, he pulled further and further away, to the point Rose barely saw him anymore - not in the way she used to. When she woke up in the mornings, he would already be gone, and she barely got more than a glimpse of him throughout the day. He was like a shadow, fleeting and quiet, barely acknowledging her anymore. She would be lucky if they even spoke a few sentences to each other some days.

Is this what marriage is really like? She thought to herself as she shifted her feet, ignoring the scowl of the painter. There was the brief honeymoon phase of love and courting, then life moved on from that whirlwind of romance and became dull. Void of love and passion. Would she be able to rekindle the romance they'd had to begin with, when everything seemed so fresh and exciting? Or was this it now - passing like shadows in the night, barely interacting. What about the baby? Maybe this child would be the key to bringing them closer together again. At least, that's what Rose hoped.

She wanted to believe that her daydreams would become reality, that the baby would bring her and Thomas together again and they would become a growing, happy family, always smiling, always together.

But as things were, it seemed her daydreams would only stay as such. She'd thought that running this hotel together would be their shared dream, their shared passion. But it seemed to have pushed them further apart than brought them closer. And the worst thing was that Rose didn't understand *why*. If there was anything bothering Thomas, he never spoke about it. He rarely divulged his real feelings, and Rose was beginning to get frustrated about the lack of communication between them these days. How could she help if she didn't understand? But every time she asked, he would brush her off, tell her he was busy with the hotel.

"And... done."

The painter's voice brought Rose out of her thoughts, and she looked up, momentarily dazed. She'd been so wrapped up in her own head she'd forgotten where she was.

"Come, take a look," the painted said, waving the brush in his hand as he grinned at them.

Thomas rose stiffly from the chair, stretching his arms over his head, and Rose forced her numb feet to move after him.

Thomas reached the easel first, peering at the portrait with a wide, beaming smile. "Oh, it's divine," he said, nodding approvingly. "Thank you, Jerod." He shook the man's hand vigorously.

Ignoring the pins and needles in her feet, Rose came up behind her husband and peered at the painting. She felt something unfamiliar tug at her chest, and her lips tightened.

Was this really what she looked like? Her eyes... they seemed so sad, so broken. Is this what Jerod saw when he looked at her? People always said that eyes were the doorway to the soul, but she'd never believed it until now. It was almost as though Jerod had seen inside her, seen the inner turmoil and sadness she felt, and painted it upon her face.

She realized, in the growing silence, that Thomas and Jerod were staring at her expectantly, and she quickly regained her composure, forcing a smile.

"It's absolutely lovely," she lied, clasping her hands together.

In reality, she found the painting rather drab. Everything about it seemed... unnatural, from the way they were positioned to the expressions on their face. Thomas's smile seemed forced even on paper, and her eyes were so round and sad. It was like he had painted a shadow of reality, a mere echo. There was no substance here. And she was sure it was because of more than the watery, monochrome color palette.

Thomas shook the painter's hand once more and led him out of the room, speaking idly between them. Rose remained where she was, her lips pursed as she continued to critique the painting.

Maybe it was merely her hormones acting up, but in some sad way, she felt like Jerod had brought her inner struggle to the surface, immortalizing it in this portrait for everyone to see. Rather than filling her with fondness, the painting would only ever remind her of her own helplessness.

She merely hoped that Thomas wouldn't notice the sadness painted on her face when the portrait was hung over their bed.

Please remember to leave a review after reading.

Follow Eve S. Evans on instagram:
@eves.evansauthor

or

@foreverhauntedpodcast

Check out our Bone-Chilling Tales to keep you awake segment on youtube for more creepy, narriated and animated haunted stories by Eve S Evans.

Let me know on Instagram that you wrote a review and I'll send you a free copy of one of my other books!

Check out Eve on a weekly basis on one of her many podcasting ventures. Forever Haunted, The Ghosts That Haunt Me with Eve Evans, Bone Chilling Tales To Keep You Awake or A Truly Haunted Podcast. (On all podcasting networks.)

If you love to review books and would like a chance to snatch up one of Eve's ARCs before publication, follow her facebook page:

Eve S. Evans Author

For exclusive deals, ARCs, and giveaways!

THE AUTHOR

From the time I was first published to current, (2021) I've learned so much about life and my journey into the paranormal.

I started this journey a few years ago after living in multiple haunted houses. However, it was one house in particular that chewed me up and spit me out you could say.

After residing in that house I wanted answers... needed them. So I began my journey of interviewing multiple people who too have been haunted. Any occuptaion, you name it, I've interviewed them.

What did I learn from my journey so far? I'm honestly not sure if I will ever get the answers I truly desire in this lifetime. However, I am determined not to stop anytime soon. I will keep plugging along, interviewing and ghost hunting. I am determined to find as many answers as I can in this lifetime before it too is my turn to be nothing but a ghost.

I have several books coming out this year and I am very well known for my "real ghost story anthologies", however, these will be mostly fictional haunted house books as I wanted to give myself a new challenge.

If you'd like to read one of my anthologies my reccomedation to start would be: True Ghost Stories of First Responders. In this book I interview police, firemen, 911 dispatchers and more. They share with me some of their creepiest calls that could possibly even be deemed "ghostly."

Also this year I am hoping to get my paranormal memoir out. I want to share my story and journey with everyone. Until then, just know that if you are terrified in your home or thinking you are going crazy with unexplained occurances, you ARE NOT alone. I thought I was going crazy too. But I wasn't.

If you'd like someone to talk to about what is going on in your home but don't know who to turn to, feel free to message me on Instagram or on Facebook.

Forever Haunted Podcast

True Whispers True Crime Podcast

Follow Eve S. Evans on instagram
@eves.evansauthor

If these walls could talk, they'd tell tales of murder

Are you ready for twisted **true** haunting stories?
Haunted houses, whether you love them or hate
them, you have to admit there's something creepy
about being in a house where a murder has taken
place.

What if you didn't know there was a murder in your
home until coming face to face with shadow people,
demonic entities, apparitions, poltergeists, or creepier
beings?

Every single haunted story in this collection will leave
you glad you're not the unfortunate soul residing in
one of these haunted houses… or are you? Get
comfortable, leave the lights on, and enjoy this
ghostly collection of stories that will send a chill up
your spine no matter how many cups of cocoa you
drink.

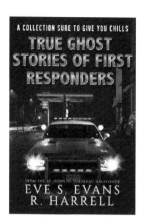

A COLLECTION SURE TO GIVE YOU CHILLS

TRUE GHOST STORIES OF FIRST RESPONDERS

FROM THE AUTHORS OF SUBURBAN HAUNTINGS

EVE S. EVANS
R. HARRELL

Don't read these spine-tingling real paranormal stories alone in the dark!

First responders with any real time on the job believe in ghosts. They've experienced events they can't otherwise explain. Same with other professions that deal with injuries, accidents, or death. Police officers, firemen, 911 operators, they've seen the worst that people can do to one another, and they've all had brushes with the unexplained.

Don't believe in ghosts? This book might change your mind steal any hope of sleep.

These stories are unexplainable, true accounts from first responders, police officers, firemen, and 911 operators, told from the perspective of everyday people. Every single tale between these covers is one hundred percent true. Think you can explain them? We dare you to try.

Abigail lost her mother—next she might lose grip on reality...

Still recovering from the loss of her mother after a punishing three-year battle with cancer, Abigail's simply stunned by her new normal. Fumbling through the motions, she learns her mother had secrets when the lawyer informs her of an unknown inheritance— a run-down mansion in the middle of nowhere.

As the only surviving heir; it's her responsibility, her inheritance, though she knew nothing of its existence.

Tired of her day job and hoping this could be a fresh start, she takes a leave of absence to visit the estate. With dreams of converting it into a bed and breakfast, she's excited for the possibilities. Unfortunately, the property is anything but a dream come true; the trouble starts with horrifying nightmares and ends with... well, unexplained paranormal experiences. Only thing is, Abigail doesn't believe in ghosts.

Until she comes face to face with one...

They wanted to go viral—now they're just hoping to survive...

Tracking Pure Evil—a podcast dedicated to the spooky things that go bump in the night—have put together a team. A team with one sole purpose; to increase their viewership by staying in the truly terrifying Redburn Manor. With over 200 years of bad luck, death, murder, suicides, accidents and absolute terror, they've found the perfect place... or so they think.

The goal? Going viral, of course.

At first, the place seems harmless; an old house with exaggerated rumors. Until late in the first day of their four-day ghost hunt when something out of the corner of someone's eye sends the group into panic mode. And those disembodied voices; are they ghosts? Or something more sinister? Never mind going viral—will they survive their stay? Or will the house swallow them?

We all wish our pets could stay with us forever... but what happens when they visit us from beyond?
This collection of true paranormal pet stories will have the hair on the back of your neck standing on end. Read accounts from owners who were certain their beloved animals came back from the other side. But don't be fooled; these stories aren't all happy reunions and love.

Some are downright chilling and might make you glad your pet hasn't come back for a visit.

If you think Pet Cemetery is scary; then these spine-tingling true accounts might just keep you awake all night long. Read at your own risk and don't say we didn't warn you.

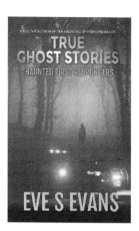

Some of the most haunting unexplained tales from 911 operators, police, firefighters, paramedics and more...

First responders with any real time on the job <u>believe in ghosts</u>. They've experienced events they can't otherwise explain. Same with other professions that deal with injuries, accidents, or death. Police officers, firemen, 911 operators, they've seen the worst that people can do to one another, and they've all had brushes with the unexplained.

Don't believe in ghosts? This book might change your mind steal any hope of sleep.

These stories are unexplainable, true accounts from first responders, police officers, firemen, and 911 operators, told from the perspective of everyday people. Every single tale between these covers is one hundred percent true. Think you can explain them? We dare you to try.

These tales of holiday hauntings will bring a bit of cheer—and fear—to your holiday season!

Are you ready to curl up with some hot cocoa, a warm blanket, and real accounts of spooky holiday hauntings? Then this is the book for you! From poor souls who moved into haunted houses to demonic encounters, poltergeist activity and more, these eerie stories will bring a bit of *boo*! to your merry and bright festivities.

Holidays are a happy time of year, but hauntings don't take the holidays off.

So curl up and dive into these disturbing tales. We recommend leaving the lights on and maybe sleeping with one eye open. After all, these paranormal encounters are all true stories. Enjoy and happy haunted-days.

Printed in Great Britain
by Amazon

76279503R00097